A GUIDE TO

A MIDSUMMER NIGHT'S DREAM

MICHAEL KERRIGAN

WITH TONY BUZAN

Hodder & Stoughton

Cover photograph ©: The Ronald Grant Archive
Mind Maps: Donna Kim-Brand
Illustrations: Karen Donnelly

Orders: please contact Bookpoint Ltd, 39 Milton Park, Abingdon, Oxon OX14 4TD.
Telephone: (44) 01235 400414, Fax: (44) 01235 400454. Lines are open from
9.00–6.00, Monday to Saturday, with a 24 hour message answering service. Email
address: orders@bookpoint.co.uk

British Library Cataloguing in Publication Data
A catalogue record for this title is available from The British Library

ISBN 0 340 66396 0

First published 1998
Impression number   11 10 9 8   7 6   5 4 3 2
Year   2004 2003 2002 2001 2000 1999 1998

The 'Teach Yourself' name and logo are registered trade marks of
Hodder & Stoughton Ltd.

Copyright © 1998 Michael Kerrigan
Introduction ('How to study') copyright © 1998 Tony Buzan

Typeset by Transet Limited, Coventry, England.
Printed in Great Britain for Hodder & Stoughton Educational, a division of
Hodder Headline Plc, 338 Euston Road, London NW1 3BH by Cox and Wyman Ltd,
Reading, Berks.

CONTENTS

There are five important things you must know about your brain and memory to revolutionise the way you study:

◆ how your memory ('recall') works *while* you are learning
◆ how your memory works *after* you have finished learning
◆ how to use Mind Maps – a special technique for helping you with all aspects of your studies
◆ how to increase your reading speed
◆ how to prepare for tests and exams.

Recall during learning
– THE NEED FOR BREAKS

When you are studying, your memory can concentrate, understand and remember well for between 20 and 45 minutes at a time. Then it needs a break. If you carry on for longer than this without a break your memory starts to break down. If you study for hours non-stop, you will remember only a small fraction of what you have been trying to learn, and you will have wasted hours of valuable time.

So, ideally, *study for less than an hour*, then take a five to ten minute break. During the break listen to music, go for a walk, do some exercise, or just daydream. (Daydreaming is a necessary brain-power booster – geniuses do it regularly.) During the break your brain will be sorting out what it has been learning, and you will go back to your books with the new information safely stored and organised in your memory banks. We recommend breaks at regular intervals as you work through the Literature Guides. Make sure you take them!

Recall after learning
— THE WAVES OF YOUR MEMORY

What do you think begins to happen to your memory straight after you have finished learning something? Does it immediately start forgetting? No! Your brain actually *increases* its power and carries on remembering. For a short time after your study session, your brain integrates the information, making a more complete picture of everything it has just learnt. Only then does the rapid decline in memory begin, and as much as 80 per cent of what you have learnt can be forgotten in a day.

However, if you catch the top of the wave of your memory, and briefly review (look back over) what you have been studying at the correct time, the memory is stamped in far more strongly, and stays at the crest of the wave for a much longer time. To maximise your brain's power to remember, take a few minutes and use a Mind Map to review what you have learnt at the end of a day. Then review it at the end of a week, again at the end of a month, and finally a week before your test or exam. That way you'll ride your memory wave all the way there – and beyond!

The Mind Map®
— A PICTURE OF THE WAY YOU THINK

Do you like taking notes? More importantly, do you like having to go back over and learn them before tests or exams? Most students I know certainly do not! And how do you take your notes? Most people take notes on lined paper, using blue or black ink. The result, visually, is boring! And what does *your* brain do when it is bored? It turns off, tunes out, and goes to sleep! Add a dash of colour, rhythm, imagination, and the whole note-taking process becomes much more fun, uses more of your brain's abilities, and improves your recall and understanding.

A Mind Map mirrors the way your brain works. It can be used for note-taking from books or in class, for reviewing what you have just studied, and for essay planning for coursework and in tests or exams. It uses all your memory's natural techniques to build up your rapidly growing 'memory muscle'.

You will find Mind Maps throughout this book. Study them, add some colour, personalise them, and then have a go at drawing your own – you'll remember them far better! Stick them in your files and on your walls for a quick-and-easy review of the topic.

HOW TO DRAW A MIND MAP

1 Start in the middle of the page. This gives your brain the maximum room for its thoughts.
2 Always start by drawing a small picture or symbol. Why? Because a picture is worth a thousand words to your brain. And try to use at least three colours, as colour helps your memory even more.
3 Let your thoughts flow, and write or draw your ideas on coloured branching lines connected to your central image. These key symbols and words are the headings for your topic. Start like the Mind Map on page 26.
4 Then add facts and ideas by drawing more, smaller, branches on to the appropriate main branches, just like a tree.
5 Always print your word clearly on its line. Use only one word per line.
6 To link ideas and thoughts on different branches, use arrows, colours, underlining, and boxes (see page 34).

HOW TO READ A MIND MAP

1 Begin in the centre, the focus of your topic.
2 The words/images attached to the centre are like chapter headings, read them next.
3 Always read out from the centre, in every direction (even on the left-hand side, where you will have to read from right to left, instead of the usual left to right).

USING MIND MAPS

Mind Maps are a versatile tool – use them for taking notes in class or from books, for solving problems, for brainstorming with friends, and for reviewing and working for tests or exams – their uses are endless! You will find them invaluable for planning essays for coursework and exams. Number your main branches in the order in which you want to use them and off you go – the main headings for your essay are done and all your ideas are logically organised!

Super speed reading

It seems incredible, but it's been proved – the faster you read, the more you understand and remember! So here are some tips to help you to practise reading faster – you'll cover the ground more quickly, remember more, and have more time left for both work and play.

◆ First read the whole text (whether it's a lengthy book or an exam or test paper) very quickly, to give your brain an overall idea of what's ahead and get it working. (It's like sending out a scout to look at the territory you have to cover – it's much easier when you know what to expect!) Then read the text again for more detailed information.

◆ Have the text a reasonable distance away from your eyes. In this way your eye/brain system will be able to see more at a glance, and will naturally begin to read faster.

◆ Take in groups of words at a time. Rather than reading 'slowly and carefully' read faster, more enthusiastically.

◆ Take in phrases rather than single words while you read.

◆ Use a guide. Your eyes are designed to follow movement, so a thin pencil underneath the lines you are reading, moved smoothly along, will 'pull' your eyes to faster speeds.

Preparing for tests and exams

◆ Review your work systematically. Cram at the start of your course, not the end, and avoid 'exam panic'!

◆ Use Mind Maps throughout your course, and build a Master Mind Map for each subject – a giant Mind Map that summarises everything you know about the subject.

◆ Use memory techniques such as mnemonics (verses or systems for remembering things like dates and events).

◆ Get together with one or two friends to study, compare Mind Maps, and discuss topics.

AND FINALLY...

Have *fun* while you learn – it has been shown that students who make their studies enjoyable understand and remember everything better and get the highest grades. I wish you and your brain every success! (Tony Buzan)

HOW TO USE THIS GUIDE

This guide assumes that you have already read *A Midsummer Night's Dream*, although you could read 'Background' and 'The story of *A Midsummer Night's Dream*' before that. It is best to use the guide alongside the play. You could read the 'Who's Who?' and 'Themes' sections without referring to the play, but you will get more out of these sections if you do refer to it to check the points made, and especially when thinking about the questions designed to test your recall and help you think about the play.

About the different sections

The 'Commentary' section can be used in a number of ways. One way is to read a scene or part of a scene in the play, and then read the commentary for that section. Keep on until you come to a test section, test yourself – and then have a break! Alternatively, read the commentary for a scene or part of a scene, then read that section in the play, then go back to the commentary. Find out what works best for you.

'Topics for discussion or brainstorming' gives topics that could well feature in exams or provide the basis for coursework. It would be particularly useful for you to discuss them with friends, or brainstorm them using Mind Map techniques (see p.v).

'How to get an "A" in English Literature' gives valuable advice on what to look for in a text, and what skills you need to develop in order to achieve your personal best.

'The exam essay' is a useful reminder of how to tackle exam questions, and 'Model answer' gives an example of an A-grade essay and the Mind Map and plan used to write it.

The questions

Whenever you come across a question with a star **O** in front of it, think about it for a moment. You could even jot down a few words in rough to focus your mind. There is not necessarily a 'right' answer to these questions: it is important for you to develop your own opinions if you want to get an 'A'. The 'Test yourself' sections are designed to take you about 10–20 minutes each – which will be time well spent. Take a short break after each one.

Line numbers

Line references are to the *Oxford World's Classics* edition, edited by Peter Holland. If you have another edition, the line numbers may be slightly different, although the act and scene numbers will normally be the same.

KEY TO ICONS

Themes

A **theme** is an idea explored by an author. Whenever a theme is dealt with in the guide, the appropriate icon is used. This means you can find where a theme is just by flicking through the book. Go on – try it now!

Love

Theatre

Authority

Perception

Change

Symbols

In addition to such clear, well-defined themes, Shakespeare also explores bigger ideas which cannot be so clearly defined. Instead, he uses **symbols**: **images** (word pictures), places even, around which different associations collect. Hence, for example, Athens in the play is, at its most straightforward level, a city, and the scene for certain parts of the action. As we read the play, however, we find that the idea of Athens suggests much more than this: notions of order, routine, reality, and other things seem to cluster round it, just as notions of disorder, disruption and dream are associated with the idea of the Wood. These symbols are discussed further in the 'How it works' chapter of the guide, and you can trace their progress through the play with the following icons:

Athens

Day

Wood

Night

STYLE AND LANGUAGE

This icon is used in the 'Commentary' wherever there is a special section on the author's choice of words and **imagery**, (the kind of word picture used to make an idea come alive).

SHAKESPEARE'S USE OF VERSE AND PROSE

Shakespeare writes in different ways in *A Midsummer Night's Dream*, according to who is speaking, and the mood they are communicating. The standard verse form, in this as in other Shakespeare plays, is the unrhymed **iambic pentameter** (or blank verse), which has five pairs of syllables to a line, the stress coming always on the second syllable. (See, for example, Act 1, scene 1, lines 214–15, where Hermia says *And in the wood where often you and I/Upon faint primrose beds were wont to lie.* ... She is recalling a vision of peaceful privacy, and the absolute regularity of these lines helps bring this impression over to her listener.) As often as not, though, Shakespeare will play about with this basic rhythm for variety or emphasis. (For instance, line 217 in the same scene starts with a stress on *There*, which gives us a sense of Hermia's resolution. The regularity of the rhythm breaks up more noticeably three lines later (220): *Farewell, sweet playfellow. Pray thou for us...*. Here, of course, Hermia is winding up her speech, about to leave, and the rhythm of her speech helps to signal this.)

There are other verse forms too, of course. The rhymed songs of Titania's fairy companions at the start of Act 2, scene 2 seem to lull us into calm, where Puck's brutally simple, short-lined, rhyming verse later (*Through the forest have I gone,/But Athenian found I none*, Act 2, scene 2, lines 73–4) suggests his unsettling quickness. In contrast, the rhyming monotony of the verse in the mechanicals' play, *Pyramus and Thisbe*, underlines its actors' lack of sophistication. Elsewhere Bottom and his friend speak in **prose** for the most part, their speech thus helping to mark out the difference between themselves and their verse-speaking social 'superiors'.

By using such a range of verse forms, then, Shakespeare keeps his play alive, and full of rhythmic variety. More than that, though, the rhythms of his verse help reflect the characters of his different speakers, and the changing moods of the play.

When and why

A Midsummer Night's Dream was written in the mid-1590s –
1595 or 1596, we are not sure which. Some experts believe it
was specially written to have its first performance, not at
Shakespeare's regular theatre, the Globe, in Southwark, London,
but in the gardens of a great country house, as the climax to the
celebrations for a big aristocratic wedding. This would certainly
have made a lot of sense. It would have meant that, as the
newly-wed King Theseus and Hippolyta, Lysander and Hermia
and Demetrius and Helena watched Bottom and his friends
performing *Pyramus and Thisbe*, they were being watched in
their turn by a real-life bride and groom! Puck, Oberon and
Titania's final blessing (Act 5, scene 1, line 363 onwards) would
then have doubled as a blessing on this young couple, their
house and their future family. As we see in the 'How it works'
chapter later, the social continuity which the institution of
marriage represents is one of the central concerns of *A
Midsummer Night's Dream*.

The social order – from top to Bottom

This social continuity is in turn part of the wider social order
which a grand country house would also have represented. A
garden setting, with flowers, grassy banks and shrubberies,
would of course have provided the perfect scene for the
woodland action of the play. More than this, though, the house,
and the garden – perhaps bordered by parkland or forest – would
have elegantly embodied the opposition between civilised Athens
and the wild Wood, upon which the play hinges.

THE ARISTOCRACY

Like any family home in Shakespearian England, such a house
would have stood for the domestic authority of the father and
the husband, and for that of the aristocratic ruling class over the
common people.

THE MONARCHY

The monarch stood in the same relation to the country as the father did to his family. Royal authority, like authority in general, was taken to be masculine by definition. That Elizabeth I, England's ruler when *A Midsummer Night's Dream* was first performed, was perhaps England's strongest, most successful monarch ever, made no difference. She herself accepted this: 'I know I have the body of a weak and feeble woman,' she once said, 'but I have the heart and stomach of a king.'

THE LOWER SOCIAL CLASSES

The house servants and peasantry – perhaps invited to stand respectfully in the background and watch this first performance from a discreet distance – were strictly subordinate, but none the less a part of the wider picture. They had to know their place in a rigid class hierarchy, but they did have a place: without their labour, the whole social structure would have come crashing down. One reason for Shakespeare's inclusion of Bottom and his friends in *A Midsummer Night's Dream* was of course the opportunity they afforded for some enjoyable comedy. Another was that their play allowed him to explore the whole question of what theatrical performance is about (see also p. 30). A third reason, though, was that this lower-class contingent completed the picture of social order that was central to the Elizabethan vision. With Bottom and his mates in place, every level of the hierarchy is present in the play. *A Midsummer Night's Dream* may seem a fantastical fairytale, but it portrays a whole society, from top to bottom.

The natural and the supernatural

A rural setting for the play's première would also have been appropriate given the closeness to ordinary country people of the natural – and the supernatural – worlds.

DO YOU BELIEVE IN FAIRIES?

An enjoyable fantasy nowadays, fairies still had a very real place in the minds of uneducated country folk in Shakespeare's time. Their fairies tended to be life-sized and mischievous (even malicious) pranksters – Puck to a T, in other words! The dinky miniaturism of Mustardseed, Mote, Peaseblossom and Cobweb represents a cute concession to the tastes of a more sophisticated audience who would not have taken the supernatural too seriously. Although Titania's tiny servitors are precisely what we think of when we think of fairies at all, this stereotype would have been new to Shakespeare's audience. Some historians think he invented the modern fairy right here, in *A Midsummer Night's Dream*. So from Tinkerbell to the fairy on the Christmas tree, it all started here!

connections between events

1 Theseus tells Hermia she must do as her father says and marry Demetrius

2 Helena tells Demetrius that Hermia intends to elope with Lysander

3 Mechanicals agree to rehearse their play in wood next night

4 Oberon and Titania quarrel

5 Oberon sees Demetrius spurn Helena; sends Puck to treat him with magic herbs

6 Oberon treats Titania with herb

7 Puck mistakenly treats Lysander

8 Lysander wakes and falls in love with Helena

9 Puck gives Bottom ass's head. Titania wakes, and falls in love with him

10 Oberon sees wrong Athenians have been treated. Sends Puck to treat Demetrius

11 Hermia and Helena quarrel; Demetrius and Lysander go to fight duel over Helena

12 Oberon brings harmony to lovers and frees Titania from spell. Bottom gets his old head back

13 Theseus says couples should all be married at same ceremony

14 Grand performance of Pyramus and Thisbe; newlyweds go to bed; Oberon, Titania and Puck bless the marriages

Act 1

Scene 1 Theseus and Hippolyta look forward to their wedding; Egeus accuses Lysander of stealing his daughter, Hermia, who is supposed to be marrying Demetrius. Theseus takes Egeus's side, but Hermia and Lysander resolve, despite this, to run away together. Their friend Helena, who herself loves Demetrius, decides to betray them. If she tells Demetrius what they are planning, she reasons, he will be grateful to her.

Scene 2 A group of Athenian tradesmen plan a performance for royal wedding celebrations; they agree to meet the following night to rehearse in a wood outside the city.

Act 2

Scene 1 Puck, jester to the Fairy King Oberon, warns a fairy servant to Queen Titania of his master's rage over the Queen's 'theft' of a boy-companion. The royal couple meet and quarrel; Oberon plans revenge and sends Puck to find a magic herb which will make the sleeping Titania fall in love with the first thing she sees on waking. Oberon then sees an Athenian youth (Demetrius) being dogged by a desperate maiden (Helena), and sends the returning Puck after them, so that the magic can be worked on the unfeeling young man as well.

Scene 2 As Titania sleeps, Oberon squeezes some juice from the herb onto her eye; meanwhile, Lysander and Hermia arrive, lost and exhausted. They decide to lie down and sleep till daylight, lying chastely apart, since they are still unmarried. Finding them like this, Puck assumes that they must be the couple his master sent him after, and he treats Lysander with the drug. As a result, when Helena now awakens him, Demetrius having finally managed to shake off her pursuit, Lysander falls head-over-heels in love with *her*. Helena assumes it's a sick joke, and runs away, but lovesick Lysander takes off after her, leaving Hermia to wake up abandoned and alone.

Act 3

Scene 1   The tradesmen have gathered in the wood to rehearse their play; Puck gives Bottom, the Weaver, an ass's head and the others flee in alarm. Titania wakes up, sees Bottom and falls instantly in love.

Scene 2   Puck is telling Oberon what he has done, but when Demetrius comes in with Hermia, who is accusing him of having murdered Lysander, it is apparent that Puck has treated the wrong couple. When Demetrius, left alone by Hermia, lies down to sleep, Puck has a second chance to get things right. This time, Helena arrives: already being pestered by Lysander, she now finds Demetrius too declaring his love. Hermia returns, accusing her of stealing Lysander's love, and Helena concludes that her former friends must have ganged up together to taunt her. As the girls quarrel, the men go off to fight a duel over Helena. Oberon tells Puck to lead the lovers off through the wood till each has been matched with his/her right partner.

Act 4

Scene 1   Taking pity on his queen, Oberon releases Titania from her spell and they are reconciled. He gives Bottom his own head back, and leaves him sleeping. Theseus, Hippolyta and Egeus arrive in the wood for a dawn hunt. They find, and wake, the sleeping young people, now perfectly matched in love: Demetrius with Helena, and Lysander with Hermia. Egeus is angry, but Demetrius says that he is happy with the way things have turned out. Theseus rules that the lovers should all be married at the same ceremony as himself and Hippolyta. Bottom wakes up, astonished, and rushes off to tell the story of his amazing dream.

Scene 2   The other workmen are agitated at the transformation of Bottom – and the resulting collapse of their venture into the field of drama. Bottom arrives, back in his old form: he has wonders to reveal, he says, but it will have to wait, since their play has been chosen for performance at the Royal Wedding celebrations.

Act 5

Scene 1 It is the evening of the next day, and the newly-weds Theseus and Hippolyta are discussing what they have been hearing about the events of the night before. Theseus is sceptical: he thinks it is all just the imagination of young love run riot. Egeus arrives with news of the entertainments on offer. Theseus plumps for the workmen's *Pyramus and Thisbe*, though Egeus tries to persuade him not to. The play goes on, and is every bit as bad as Egeus has predicted, but it is none the less good-humouredly received. Theseus draws the celebrations to a close, and the mortals go off to bed, leaving the stage to Oberon, Titania and Puck, who bless the house and promise their protection to the newly married couples.

HOW MUCH CAN YOU REMEMBER?

Try to fill in the missing words from this alternative summary without looking back at the original. Feel free to use your own words if they have the same meaning.

Act 1

Scene 1 Theseus and Hippolyta look forward to their
_____ ; Egeus accuses Lysander of stealing his daughter,
_____ , who is, he says, supposed to be marrying _____ .
Theseus takes Egeus's side, but the young lovers decide to run away together. Their friend _____ resolves to betray them to
_____ .

Scene 2 Some tradesmen plan to rehearse a play. They will meet next night in the _____ outside the city.

Act 2

Scene 1 Puck, jester to the Fairy King _____ , says his master is furious with Queen _____ . The King and Queen meet and quarrel; the King plans revenge and sends Puck to find a _____ which will make the sleeping Queen fall in love with the first thing she sees when she wakes up. The King

sees an Athenian youth (_____) dogged by a desperate
maiden (_____) and decides to help.

Scene 2 As Titania sleeps, Oberon squeezes juice from the
herb on her eye; meanwhile, _____ and Hermia, lost and
exhausted, lie down and sleep. Finding them, _____ assumes
they must be the couple his master wanted him to treat with
the herb, so he anoints _____ 's eyes with the drug. When
_____ arrives and wakes him, Demetrius having finally
managed to shake off her pursuit, _____ falls head-over-
heels in love with *her*. They go off, and _____ is left
all alone.

Act 3

Scene 1   The tradesmen are in the wood rehearsing their play;
Puck gives _____ an ass's head and the others flee in fear.
Titania wakes, sees him and falls in love.

Scene 2   Puck tells _____ what he has done, but when
Demetrius comes in with _____ , who is accusing him of
having murdered Lysander, it becomes clear that Puck has
treated the wrong couple. Left alone by Hermia, Demetrius lies
down to sleep, so Puck has a second chance to get things
right. This time, _____ arrives: already being pestered by
Lysander, she now finds Demetrius too declaring his love.
Hermia returns, saying her old friend has stolen Lysander's
love, and _____ concludes that her former friends must have
joined together to taunt her. As the girls quarrel, the men go off
to fight a duel over Helena. Oberon tells _____ to lead the
lovers off through the wood till each has been matched with
his/her right partner.

Act 4

Scene 1   Taking pity, _____ releases Titania from her spell.
He gives _____ his own head back, leaving him sleeping.
_____ , Hippolyta and Egeus arrive in the wood for a dawn
hunt. They find the young people, now perfectly matched in
love: Demetrius with _____ , and Lysander with _____ .
Egeus is angry, but _____ rules that the lovers should share a

wedding with himself and Hippolyta. Bottom wakes up, astonished.

Scene 2 The other workmen are agitated at the transformation of Bottom, but he promptly arrives, back in his old form: he has wonders to reveal, he says, but it will have to wait, since their play, _____ *and* _____ , has been chosen for performance at the Royal Wedding celebrations.

Act 5

Theseus and _____ are talking about the strange stories they have heard about the events of the night before. Egeus tells him the entertainments on offer and Theseus plumps for *Pyramus and* _____ . The play is performed, then Theseus draws the celebrations to a close and the mortals go to bed, leaving the stage to Oberon, Titania and _____ , who bless the newly married couples.

now that you've got the plot, take a break before finding out who's who

WHO'S WHO?

The Mini Mind Map above summarises the character groups in *A Midsummer Night's Dream.* Test yourself by looking at the full Mind Map on p. 19, and then copying the Mini Mind Map and trying to add to it from memory.

HOW TO REMEMBER WHO'S WHO

It can be hard at first to tell which character is which in *A Midsummer Night's Dream,* so think of nicknames that will help you do the job. The young lovers seem more or less interchangeable at first, though the distinctions are crucial and with time will become clear. There is all the difference in the world between Lyrical Lysander and Dour Demetrius. Of the girls, meanwhile, Hapless Helena has a *Hell*ish time for much of the play, whereas everyone seems to want Heavenly Hermia. Aged Egeus is Hermia's possessive pa. It is harder to think of nicknames for Theseus and Hippolyta, but then it's harder to forget who they are. And while it isn't easy to remember which workman is which, you don't really have to, since they form a company of equals, none of whom takes on any strongly individual identity. Except, of course, for Bottom, and if you can't remember his name then you really have got problems!

Noble mortals

Theseus

The Duke of Athens, Theseus is a brisk, businesslike man, used to power and authority. He embodies the world of the daytime city – a world of law, order and matter-of-fact clarity. It is significant that he will not enter the night-time wood which is the setting for the play's main enchanted action. Instead, the arrival of his hunting party (Act 4, scene 1) will signal the restoration of daytime order. Theseus's problem is that he lacks imagination. It is ironic, then, that this down-to-earth detachment should enable him to give the play's most thoughtful (and, in its firmly anti-poetic way, poetic) summary of what the imagination involves and is capable of (Act 5, scene 1, lines 4–22).

It is ironic, too, that *Pyramus and Thisbe*, the play within the play of *A Midsummer Night's Dream*, is conceived, written and finally staged in Theseus's honour. Like any government, Theseus has an arts policy: he senses that events and spectacles are essential to a society's sense of itself. He recognises the importance of entertainments, even though he himself may not be able to enter imaginatively into the darker, more thrilling and more disturbing dimensions that art opens up.

Hippolyta

Theseus's bride-to-be, Hippolyta, is not the easiest of characters to pin down. Not that you have to, of course: her ambiguity only makes her more interesting. She doesn't seem obviously upset in Act 1, scene 1 at the prospect of marrying Theseus (though there could be a hint in lines 7–8 that the time which is passing so slowly for Theseus cannot pass slowly enough for her). It is worth bearing in mind, though, that the marriage with Theseus was not her idea. In Greek mythology Hippolyta was the Queen of the Amazons, a race of fiercely independent women warriors who rejected men. They were finally defeated in battle by the forces of Theseus – so Hippolyta comes to the Duke as a trophy of war. Her marriage to him symbolises her own surrender, and her man-hating nation's subjection, to the authority of Theseus and Athens. (Theseus touches on this in Act 1, scene 1, lines 116–17.)

What this says about the play's view of love and marriage is a matter of interpretation. On the one hand you could argue that Shakespeare presents the Amazons' self-sufficiency – and hence female chastity in general – as a barren, fruitless, self-centred state that must be brought to an end, by force if necessary. Theseus certainly speaks of it in these terms to Hermia, Act 1, scene 1, lines 72, 74. How is humankind to continue, after all, if women refuse to have children? On the other hand, you could see the play as highlighting the oppression of women by men, presenting marriage as a straightforward subjection of women, backed up by law and the threat of force.

Egeus

If Theseus represents the authority of the state and the law, Hermia's father Egeus stands for paternal authority within the family. But just as the limitations of Theseus's worldly order will be highlighted by the revelation of a parallel realm of dream and magic, in which his earthbound authority is not recognised, Egeus too will have to accept that his power over his daughter has its limits. His is a possessive, even savage love – in Act 1, scene 1, line 44 he makes it clear he is prepared to contemplate the idea of his daughter's death rather than accept her disobedience. ✪ Do you think she owes him any obedience at all?

This paternal authority is upheld by Theseus as the play begins, but then, as Egeus's own language makes clear (Act 1, scene 1, lines 97–8), wider principles of property and law are at stake – what will happen to the fabric of society if its daughters are going to start disposing of themselves in marriage, making a nonsense of any contractual agreements their fathers may have made? By Act 4, scene 1, though, Demetrius is waiving his claim to Hermia, these principles are no longer threatened, and the Duke supports Hermia's marriage with Lysander. *Egeus, I will overbear your will*, he says (Act 4, scene 1, line 178). Sometimes what a character does not say can be as crucial as what he or she does, and

Egeus's silence on this decision is deafening. Like it or not, though, he must give way to a public authority higher than his own private authority.

Hermia

In the romantic comedy which makes up the heart of *A Midsummer Night's Dream*, Hermia seems to have things pretty much her own way: she is loved by the man she herself loves, Lysander – and, indeed, by another man she doesn't: Helena's love, Demetrius. It can be hard to remember as the play goes on that when we first meet Hermia she is under the threat of death or confinement in a convent. For Hermia, though, the play can be seen as a progression from the role of young girl, under her father's authority, to that of grown woman, able to choose her own husband. Cynics will say that this represents a move from one form of subjection to another – especially if Oberon's crushing of Titania's will (see Titania, on p. 16) is taken as the play's model for marriage. The truth is, of course, that Shakespeare is never as simple as that. You can see these things either way, and in any case, both Hermia and Titania are living, breathing characters: they cannot be reduced to mere symbols of any single view of the world.

Lysander

As a high-born young man, Hermia's love Lysander has much invested in his self-image as a gentleman and as a courtly lover. He has mastered the language of romantic love almost too well, only forgetting that the true knight shows his love, finally, not by his words but by the deeds he does in the service and protection of his maiden.

This idea of himself will be undercut in Act 3, scene 1 when, under the influence of Puck's magic, Lysander finds himself behaving in a most ungentlemanly way to the supposed eternal object of his love, Hermia. The high-flown language of Lysander's love is placed under particular scrutiny then. It loses much of its credibility once it becomes clear that it can be turned out by the yard, and that it consists of praises so preposterously superlative that it leaves the real woman behind and addresses only an abstract ideal.

While Hermia and Helena are two different individuals, as far as the language of love is concerned they seem interchangeable, and while the terms it uses for them are flattering (see Act 3, scene 2, both Lysander's and Demetrius's speeches), they do not convey much about the reality of either woman.

Helena

Of all the young lovers, Helena is the one who seems most to resist the wood's spell. She is the only one who does not at any point in the night fall asleep – which in the other characters can be seen as marking the moment of victory for the wood's magic powers. Helena has good reason for her more realistic attitude, though, having been so thwarted to begin with. It is as though the earlier loss of Demetrius's love leaves Helena literally 'disenchanted' and therefore unenchantable: she starts off in despair where Demetrius, Lysander and Hermia all enter the wood in hope of one thing or another. It is ironic that, as the night approaches its end, she will be the one whose midsummer night's dream has come true: having the love of both young men she finds herself in Hermia's former situation, which she found so enviable in Act 1, scene 1, line 191. However, it doesn't give her what she wanted.

Demetrius

Although the least clearly individuated of the young Athenians, Demetrius does develop during the course of the play. Though in Act 1, scene 1 he claims to love Hermia, the way he demands her as if in completion of a deal does not suggest strong feelings on his part – and shows complete indifference to any feelings she might have herself. But this egotism is imprisoning. So long as he is in thrall to it, the love of another person is no more than an irritating nuisance – hence the bitter near-violence of his treatment of Helena in Act 2, scene 1. Puck's magic frees him from his own selfishness, allowing him to appreciate the value of the love Helena offers him, and through that discover depths in his own character. The Demetrius who speaks so lovingly of Helena and so wonderingly of his night's experiences at the end of Act 4, scene 2 is not the cold, legalistic speaker of Act 1, scene 1.

Fairies

Oberon

Theseus's counterpart in Fairyland, King Oberon, is also the presiding genius behind the enchanted action in the night-time wood. He attempts to work the other characters like the cast in his own little play. His spells are responsible for the action we see, making a spectacle of the Queen with Bottom and organising the romantic lives of Hermia, Lysander, Helena and Demetrius. In that sense, he can be seen as a playwright within the play, a stand-in for Shakespeare. The difference, of course, is that Oberon is nothing like so skilled a dramatist. Though he produces an amusing (if unsophisticated) comedy in the case of Titania and Bottom, the joyous romantic comedy he envisages for the young Athenians ends up in a hopeless tangle. Like the author of *Pyramus and Thisbe*, Oberon teaches us how not to write a play – and so helps us better to appreciate the all-but-magical accomplishment behind a play that really works.

The ultimate proof of Oberon's inadequacy as a playwright is his inability to stomach his own creation. As we shall see in Act 4, scene 1, line 48, when he calls the innocent Bottom 'hateful', Oberon cannot actually endure the sight of his queen with the monster his assistant has created. By line 74, however, Oberon has clearly moved beyond such negative notions as that of hatefulness anyway. In much more positive mood he calls on Titania to *Be as thou wast wont to be,/ See as thou wast wont to see* (lines 70–1). These lines imply an acceptance of Titania exactly 'as she was' – faults and all. Oberon, who thought that he was the one dishing out the magic during this night of enchantment, has himself been changed by the experience –though the change, ironically, is to an acceptance of how things were to begin with!

Titania

Though so many of the play's main characters stand on the brink of marriage, and their wedding celebrations will indeed constitute its conclusion, Titania and Oberon's is actually the play's only real, up-and-running marriage. Not that they are much of a role-model! The Fairyland action opens (Act 2, scene 1) with the royal couple so much at odds that they have separated, and while it will conclude with their loving reconciliation (Act 4, scene 1), the means by which that reconciliation has been brought about are questionable, to say the least.

A wilful, wayward wife, Titania disobeys her husband and is punished with humiliation. We should not let the humour of her dalliance with Bottom blind us to the cruelty of her punishment. Magnanimous as Oberon may feel by Act 4, scene 1, he was not prepared to take this view until he had won Titania's surrender (line 57). Marital harmony, according to this view of Oberon's behaviour, depends strictly on the man's remaining in charge. Thus the royal marriage in Fairydom raises the same issues as its Athenian equivalent (see Hippolyta, p. 12). Is marriage about equal sharing or dominance and submission? ✪ What do you think?

Puck

General factotum to the Fairy King, Puck embodies the spirit of mischief in Fairyland. Shakespeare took this character directly from the folk tradition, in which from time immemorial he had worked his wicked pranks. Puck was also often called Robin Goodfellow – in a spirit partly of fearful flattery (if they were nice enough about him, people hoped, he might spare them his attentions), and partly, too, of **irony**, given that, far from being a 'good fellow', he was a thoroughly bad lot. (In much the same spirit, of course, modern American gangsters have been referred to as 'goodfellas'.) The Puck of *A Midsummer Night's Dream* is true to tradition. Along with an undoubted sense of humour, he also has a distinctly cruel streak, as the practical joke he describes in Act 2, scene 1, lines 46–57, for instance, illustrates. The misery caused to the mortal lovers when his plan unravels upsets Oberon: as far as Puck is concerned, however, it just makes things that much more fun (Act 3, scene 2, lines 352–3). In addition to all his other faults, Puck is a snob, describing the workmen in Act 3, scene 2, lines 9–10 as *A crew of patches, rude mechanicals*. The fact that they *work for bread upon Athenian stalls* damns them in his eyes – though we might rather respect them for it.

The venom with which Puck talks here is on the face of it surprising: what did these inoffensive souls ever do to him? The answer perhaps lies in his own peculiar status. His supernatural powers may be phenomenal, but he remains a servant. Theseus, Hippolyta and the young lovers are all of high, if human, birth, and all have been taken under the protection of the Fairy King. These *rude mechanicals*, as Puck calls them (Act 3, scene 2, line 9), are perhaps the only characters in the play to whom he can feel securely superior.

Bottom and the mechanicals

The *mechanicals* can be seen as constituting a single collective character – it is not just that Shakespeare has not made the effort to mark them each out as individuals (though it is for the most part true, he hasn't). Rather, as can be seen in the informal, democratic way in which they rehearse their play (Act 1, scene 2; Act 3, scene 1), these working-class men seem naturally to operate as a team, all for one and one for all. Bottom is the most (if not the only) developed individual character among them, and it is clear from Act 4, scene 2 that his mates look up to him as someone special.

To us, of course, just about everything about Bottom can seem absurd, from his name to his lack of education, to his swaggering sense of his own importance. Yet the man who wants 'Bottom's Dream' to be made into a ballad with himself as hero (Act 4, scene 1, lines 210–12) has worthwhile qualities too. There is something comic about his concern that his fairy servitor should not be overwhelmed by the contents of the humble-bee's honeybag he has sent him to fetch (Act 4, scene 1, lines 14–16), but there is also something touching. Low-born, vulgar and grossly physical as he admittedly is, Bottom displays a native nobility which his social 'betters' do not always match.

now that you know your Helena from your Hermia, take a break before seeing how it all fits together

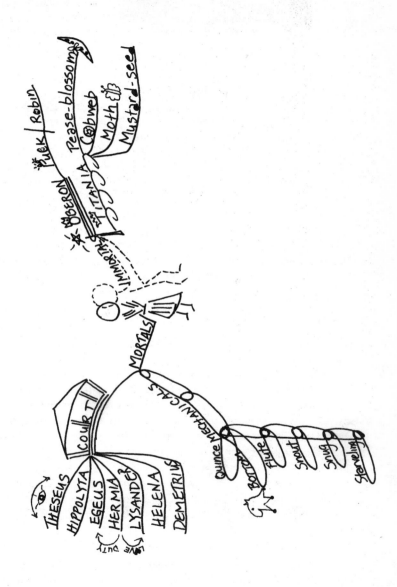

OW IT WORKS: STRUCTURE

Although the action in *A Midsummer Night's Dream* keeps moving excitingly along through all five acts, it is none the less noticeable that the serious drama reaches its conclusion long before the play proper does. As early as Act 3, scene 2, lines 394–5 Oberon makes clear his intentions of bringing everything out all right. The action of Act 4 is accordingly devoted to the release of Titania from her humiliating delusion and the untangling of the knots the young lovers have been left in – first, by Demetrius's perverse spurning of Helena and turning to Hermia, and second, by Puck's misguided intervention. Act 5 largely consists of a happy reunion of the cast, finding both young lovers and mechanicals back in Athens, where the groups will have their only meeting as actors and audience at the court of Theseus, under the benevolent protection of the Fairy King and Queen.

A CIRCULAR ARGUMENT

So if the drama is over only half-way through the play, why does the whole thing not simply fall flat? Usually, we know, a dramatist tries to build tension as the play goes on, till it reaches its end in a smashing climax. *A Midsummer Night's Dream*, though, does not present things in such a 'linear' fashion. While obviously, as in any play, the action has to be staged as a series of events taking place one after another in time, the dynamic energy of this play pushes in quite a different direction. The emotional heart of *A Midsummer Night's Dream* is its structural heart, its centre. The concentric circles of Figure 1 (p. 21) tell us much more about the progress of the play than any linear plot summary could.

DAY 1 ATHENS V. NIGHT/WOOD

In the diagram the outer circle represents the daytime world of Athens, a state of disciplined order and down-to-earth reality. The inner circle represents the night-time wood, Oberon's

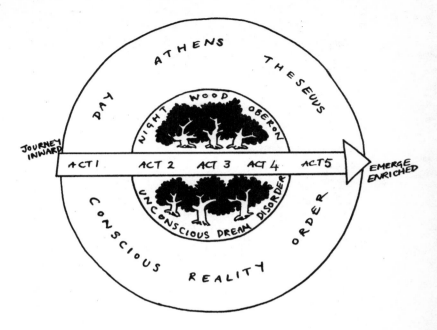

Figure 1

kingdom – a dark realm of disorder and away-with-the-fairies fantasy. Psychologically, the move from Athens to the wood can be seen as an inward journey from the conscious to the unconscious level. Though the irredeemably rational, orderly Theseus has to remain in the outer zone throughout, with Hippolyta and Egeus, the other two main groups among the mortals – the ardent young lovers and the innocent, unsophisticated mechanicals – both go into the wood and have their very different experiences of it. Emerging during Act 4, they find themselves right back where they started, in Athens, unsure as they return groggily to consciousness whether their journey has taken place at all. It has though, we know. For one thing, the tangled affections of Hermia, Lysander, Helena and Demetrius have sorted themselves out as if by magic. For another, the Athens of Act 5 is a subtly different place from the Athens of Act 1: there is an energy, a crackling charge in Act 5, scene 1 that wasn't there before. At its most basic you can see it as the sexual tension of three couples on the brink of their first marital bedtime. More than this, though, it is a mark of how the conscious, everyday level of life is enhanced by any touch of enchantment – whether the magic comes in the form of actual spells or in their equivalents: romantic love, dream or, as in *A Midsummer Night's Dream*, art.

OPPOSITES AT WORK

Figure 2, on p. 23, shows some of the oppositions at work in *A Midsummer Night's Dream* between these two symbolic orders of existence: Theseus's world of daytime Athens and Oberon's night-time wood. These oppositions are not of course presented anything like so baldly in Shakespeare's text (you can trace them through the action by the Athens, Wood, Day and Night icons in the Commentary section) but it is none the less revealing to view them as they are laid out here, for they are important underlying principles in *A Midsummer Night's Dream*. It is another aspect of the play's non-linearity that it does not move simply from one side of the table to the other – from the conscious to the unconscious, say, or vice-versa – but holds both simultaneously in suspension, finding each indispensable to life.

SHAKESPEARIAN CYCLES

You cannot, Shakespeare's play suggests, have clear, matter-of-fact consciousness without a dark, dreamy unconscious, any more than you can have day without night. The dominant movement in *A Midsummer Night's Dream* is thus not one of progression from start to finish but of cycles: the never-ending cycles of the sun that give us days and nights; the phases of the moon that mark out our months; the seasons of the year. And, of course, the wider cycles by which men and women are born, grow up and die having brought into the world meanwhile the new babies of generations to come. See Figure 3 – The Bard on a Bike, p. 24.

CONSCIOUS	UNCONSCIOUS
LIGHT	DARK
REALITY	DREAM
CLARITY	MYSTERY
OPENNESS	CONCEALMENT
ORDER	DISORDER
LAW	LICENCE
DUTY	DESIRE
ROUTINE	DISRUPTION
MUNDANE	MAGIC
LIFE	ART
PROSE	POETRY

Figure 2

LIFE GOES ON

Such cycles are central, not merely to *A Midsummer Night's Dream*, but to Shakespearian comedy in general. Comedy isn't all laughs, nor does it necessarily even involve more light than dark. The point is rather that it reassures us that life goes on. Death is not absent from the world of comedy, it is just that in this world it leads to rebirth, as night does to day. These

Figure 3 Bard on a bike

continuities are collective. Each of us individually may grow old and die, but society survives. The life of the individual is finite, will end in that individual's death, and is therefore tragic. (Think of Shakespeare's great tragedies, for the most part each named for a single person – *Hamlet, Othello, King Lear,* or *Macbeth*.) Comedy, by contrast, celebrates the endurance of the community. That is why, instead of building suspense or tension in a linear narrative, *A Midsummer Night's Dream* seems to go round in circles, and ends – since it must, as a stageplay, end somewhere – not with some dramatic confrontation but with an act of collective celebration which brings together all levels of society, from the lowest to the highest – even the immortals.

now relax and give yourself a chance to unwind a little – or you'll end up going round in circles yourself!

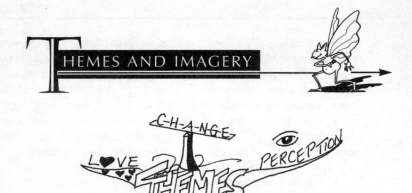

A theme is an idea developed or explored throughout a work. The main themes of *A Midsummer Night's Dream* are shown in the Mini Mind Map above. 'Imagery' refers to the kind of word picture used to bring the themes to life. Test yourself on the themes by copying the Mini Mind Map above, adding to it yourself, and then comparing your results with the full Mind Map on p. 34.

Love

Love, they say, makes the world go round, and since, as we saw in the previous section, *A Midsummer Night's Dream* is a play built around cycles, that is appropriate enough. Without the love that leads men and women to come together, produce and rear families, the world – as far as the human race is concerned at any rate – would grind to a halt. The love that underpins the institution of marriage comprises both desire and devotion. Without the first, men and women would never produce new children; the second is essential if those children are to be successfully raised in their turn. Love within the family comes in different forms, of course. Egeus's paternal love for his daughter Hermia is tied up with ideas of authority, duty and law; in Act 1, scene 1, lines 150–5 Hermia will turn the tables, presenting the love she feels for Lysander as a law unto itself.

Both are right in a sense. You must consider for yourself how far Hermia is right to follow the law of love. Arguably, Egeus has a right to require his daughter's obedience until she is old enough to make her own mind up; and she has a right to leave her immediate family for the man she loves when she is sure that it is time to do so.

LOVE AND DUTY

For society's sake, love does have to submit to discipline: comic as it is, Titania's infatuation with the modified Bottom offers a more serious warning, too, of what monstrosities might come about if certain boundaries are not observed. At the same time, though, love has to have the courage to break a few rules. If every girl in Hermia's position were meekly to submit to her father's natural possessiveness, the human race would die out. So it has always been: love winning out, but never without a struggle.

LOVE AND CONFLICT

But then conflict and love go hand in hand. If good marriages, like good friendships, involve mutual respect and co-operation, they can also involve possessiveness and jealousy – negative feelings which deform closeness and affection. The best of friendships, meanwhile, can be undermined by love. See how the good-hearted Helena starts plotting against her friend Hermia at the end of Act 1, scene 1 – and how Helena in her turn complains of Hermia's betrayal during their quarrel in the wood (Act 3, scene 2, lines 192–344).

LOVE AND POETRY

Love is traditionally associated with poetry, too, with high-flown compliments and extravagant vows. As Lysander's example so often shows, however, these can take flight to such an extent that the language of love is emptied of meaning. In Act 3, scene 2, we see how Hermia and Helena become to all intents and purposes interchangeable in the language of Demetrius and Lysander: the young men's compliments are so ridiculously poetic that they will do either woman equally well – or badly. Likewise we see how the terms in which Lysander expresses his 'false' love – the feelings Puck's magic have given him for Helena – are indistinguishable from those in which he expresses his 'true' love for Hermia. Amid all this rhetoric, the beloved herself is all but forgotten – as Lysander's beloved Hermia finds herself forgotten in Act 2, scene 2, lines 151–62.

ROMANTIC CHALLENGES

Yet where the challenge the play faces Lysander with is that of bringing his love back down to earth, from the realm of empty eloquence to that of living, breathing life, the task for Demetrius, as we saw in his 'Who's who?' entry on p. 15, is to acquire a bit of romance. He has to learn to stop seeing love as a glorified business deal. His wondering thought, in Act 4, scene 1, lines 186–7, that the things he now sees around him seem *Like far-off mountains turnèd into clouds*, shows us that, along with a true appreciation of Helena and her love, he has gained a new way of looking at his world. True love changes us, as it does both Lysander and Demetrius, helping us reach beyond our normal limitations to our 'better selves'.

Authority

Authority takes a number of different forms in *A Midsummer Night's Dream*. The play calls into question the authority of the King (Theseus) over his subjects, of the state (Athens) over its citizens, of the father (Egeus) over his child (Hermia), of the husband (Oberon) and his wife (Titania). The elopement of Hermia and Lysander represents a defiance of the first three of these (King, State and Father). Titania's refusal to return the Indian boy is a rejection of the fourth. The crazy goings-on in the night-time wood can be seen as upsetting any idea of order or authority altogether. ❂ How far is this really the case? The Queen is, of course, humiliatingly punished for her waywardness – but Hermia, surely, is rewarded for hers? So it may seem at first glance.

WHO WEARS THE TROUSERS?

More carefully considered, though, things are not so simple. While the play may appear to approve of Hermia's romantic rebellion, she will end up subjecting herself to the authority of another man, her husband Lysander, in marriage. It is true that the men in *A Midsummer Night's Dream* do not always wear the trousers: the romantic tradition of poetic love does confer on the lady an authority of her own – though on a strictly temporary basis. But the Demetrius and Lysander who so exaggeratedly abase themselves to Helena in Act 3, scene 2 will probably be just as bad as Oberon once they are married!

BACK TO REALITY

Revelling as it does in the suspension of everyday order, in magical transformations and escape into dream, *A Midsummer Night's Dream* none the less has its thematic feet firmly on the ground. The disorder of the night-time wood is liberating, but the lovers must return to the real world to live their lives, just as we have to return from the exhilarating heights of artistic fantasy to the more mundane concerns of everyday life. The trick is to enhance the life we have, not to change it altogether.

As we saw in 'How it works' on p. 20, *A Midsummer Night's Dream* sees order and disorder as two sides of the same coin. Rules are made to be broken – but only so that the wider principle of order should be maintained. Though some scholars have looked to Shakespeare for radical political messages, they have by and large been disappointed. *A Midsummer Night's Dream*, too, is more conservative than it may immediately seem. Feminists may be inclined to applaud the Amazonian independence of Hippolyta, Hermia's daughterly disobedience and Titania's feisty insubordination. However, they will be less happy at the thought that Hippolyta is effectively a trophy of war, that Hermia ends up meekly marrying and that Titania is crushed once more into wifely submission.

In the same way, those who have felt that the mechanicals represent some sort of revolutionary spirit are also, surely, misguided. There is, undoubtedly, a real sense of energy about Bottom and his friends – and they do, among themselves, show a splendidly democratic spirit of mutual loyalty and co-operation. There is never, however, the slightest hint that they hold their social 'superiors' in anything other than the highest, most unquestioning regard.

Change

The idea of change is central to *A Midsummer Night's Dream*. The characters are, as we have seen, forced by their experiences to change in their views of themselves and each other. Magic changes reality in the wood, throwing the ordinary rules of nature into disorder, allowing Puck (Act 2, scene 1, lines 175–6) to *put a girdle round about the earth /in forty minutes,* giving a man an ass's head and making a nonsense of the normal scale of things (think of Bottom and his fairy servitors in Act 3, scene 1 and Act 4, scene 1, for instance). The poet works magical change when, like Shakespeare in *A Midsummer Night's Dream,* he weaves a world out of words and, as Theseus puts it (Act 5, scene 1, lines 16–17), *gives to airy nothing/ A local habitation and a name.*

IMAGES AND SPELLS

As we see in our discussion of Act 2, scene 1 in the Commentary later on, the images which change flowers into soldiers or dewdrops into pearls, can themselves be seen as spells of a sort. But then so too can the whole theatrical experience. What is it if not magic that changes a modern actor into an Athenian nobleman, a 'rude mechanical' or an Amazon queen? If we are prepared to co-operate ourselves, to play our own part as audience by using our imagination, the magic they work may even change our lives a little.

Theatre

A Midsummer Night's Dream is a work of theatre – that is obvious enough. But it is also a work *about* theatre. We saw in the preceding section how the play can be seen to highlight the wizardry of writing, the magical powers of performance. In that sense the play can be seen to celebrate the wonder of art and the theatre. It should also be noticed, however, that Shakespeare's play actually contains one play in performance – the mechanicals' production of *Pyramus and Thisbe*. And as we have seen in looking at Oberon (p. 16), the Fairy King's attempts to manipulate the action in the wood can be seen as a second. Each of these different plays-within-the-play highlights by its clumsiness the all but magical accomplishment of a real playwright like Shakespeare, and the skills involved in bringing a classic drama to the stage: lighting, music, costume and scenery as well as direction and acting.

THEATRE AND SOCIETY

Preposterous as it is, *Pyramus and Thisbe* does demonstrate some of the benefits of the theatre: its social value as an activity which brings a community together, whether as audience or as actors, and the opportunities it offers for even those of relatively little education, like Bottom and his friends, to extend horizons otherwise bounded by work. Even the resolutely unimaginative Theseus is aware of this aspect of theatre's importance.

More than a stage-play, *A Midsummer Night's Dream* is a glorious tribute to the theatre as a whole – to the whole strange business of writing, rehearsal, interpretation, direction, to the magic, living communication between actors and audience. This is why the mechanicals' farcical tragedy should not be dismissed as a trivial 'comic subplot', thrown in just to lighten the mood. On the contrary, it is the central performance of a play about plays.

Perception

Reality is perceived in *A Midsummer Night's Dream* – as in life – by the five bodily senses. Any dramatic performance must of course appeal to the senses of sight and hearing, but Shakespeare's language in this play thrills the mind's eye too, with images of cowslip soldiers and dewdrop pearls (Act 2, scene 1, lines 10, 14–15), and fans made of butterfly-wings (Act 3, scene 2, lines 163–4), to mention only a few of the poetry's visual miracles. Music is crucial to this play, but our ears are delighted by Shakespeare's verse as well: not just its rhythms but at times, as in Oberon's *I know a bank* speech (Act 2, scene 1, lines 249–56), in the very sound of the words. With all its fragrant flowers, that speech appeals to our sense of smell too, as well as to the sense of touch (the warmth and luxurious softness of Titania's couch; the snake's sudden chillness). In Act 3, scene 1, lines 157–9, the Fairy Queen orders her servants to bring Bottom a selection of mouthwatering delicacies, appealing to our sense of taste.

REALITY V. ILLUSION

We do not only perceive physically, however. As we saw earlier, Theseus is the play's leading realist. An intelligent but determinedly unimaginative observer, he perceives his prosaic world with complete clarity. Where Theseus uses his head, the other main characters lose theirs. Thinking 'with the heart', they leap over the boundaries of 'factual' reality into a very different realm of experience. A realm not of objective 'truth' but illusion, it is for all that a world of wonder; though it may not be 'real' itself, it has the capacity to transform reality.

Love takes the young lovers into an ecstatic world beyond humdrum reality. It enables Demetrius and Lysander in particular to transcend their usual limitations and attain their 'better selves'. Magic and dream are external forces in the night-time wood, but their effect on the young people is much the same. As for us, as readers or audience, we are not ourselves involved in the characters' story. Yet art, in the form of Shakespeare's play, allows us an experience every bit as magical, every bit as transcendent.

MUSIC AND POETRY

The song and dance in which *A Midsummer Night's Dream* abounds makes it an audiovisual feast, bombarding its audience's senses as well as addressing its mind. It is always important for poetry to appeal to the senses as well as the intellect. But it is especially important in a play which concerns the need to transcend everyday reality, to cross the frontiers of normal thought into the realms of dream and magic.

We are used to language explaining all mystery, all strangeness away, reducing everything to cold common sense. The task the creative writer faces is to help language conquer this side of its own nature, helping us not merely to understand our world but to appreciate its wonder. One of the great gifts of the theatre is that it is not bound by its binding as a book is. The written script is only the start: in performance, the play offers not just words and their meanings but actors, voices, sounds, scenery, spectacle.

HEAD V. HEART

So though it may seem an odd thing to say of a classic work of literature, words in *A Midsummer Night's Dream* are almost a necessary evil. We have to use words, but we will attempt to use them in a way that speaks not to the 'head' but to the 'heart'. Shakespeare reaches beyond the immediate meaning of his words to exploit the music inherent in language – the rhythms of prose and poetry (in a variety of different line-lengths and rhyme schemes), the sounds of the words themselves – as well as music proper, sometimes just instrumental, sometimes integrated with his poetry in the form of songs. He seduces the mind with the smells of woodland herbs and flowers, appeals to the sense of touch with his talk of soft beds, gentle breezes – and, on the other hand, chilly serpents. Sound, rhythm and spectacle, all contribute to the effects of the fairies' dances.

All in all, *A Midsummer Night's Dream* is an astonishingly vivid and varied multimedia experience. Not just a great work of art, it is a celebration of art itself.

now put down your Shakespeare and get some exercise, or put on some music – or bombard your senses with a cup of tea and a biscuit!

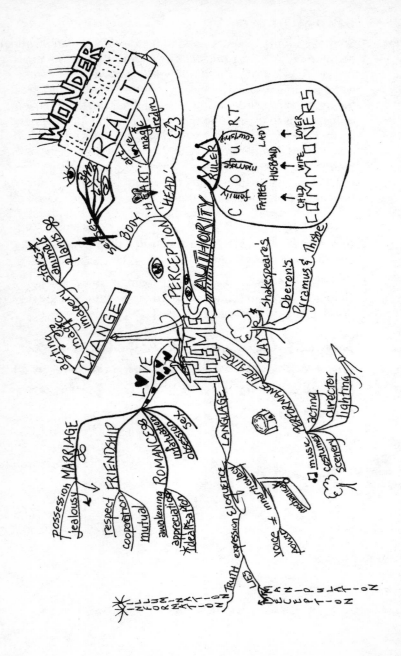

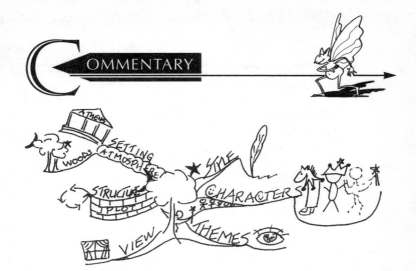

COMMENTARY

The Commentary looks at each scene in turn, beginning with a brief preview which will prepare you for the scene and help in last-minute revision. The Commentary comments on whatever is important in the section, focusing on the areas shown in the Mini Mind Map above.

ICONS

Wherever there is a focus on a particular theme, the icon for that theme appears in the margin (see p. xi for key). Look out, too, for the 'Style and language' sections. Being able to comment on style and language will help you to get an 'A' in your exam. You will learn more from the Commentary if you use it alongside the play itself. Read a scene from the play, then the corresponding Commentary section – or the other way around.

QUESTIONS

Remember that when a question appears in the Commentary with a star ✪ in front of it, you should stop and think about it for a moment. And do **remember to take a break** after completing each exercise!

Act 1 scene 1

◆ Theseus and Hippolyta look forward to their wedding.
◆ Egeus accuses Lysander of stealing his daughter Hermia, who has been promised to Demetrius.
◆ Theseus takes Egeus's side, but Hermia and Lysander resolve to run away together.
◆ Helena, who herself loves Demetrius, decides to betray Hermia and Lysander in order to win Demetrius's gratitude.

Though the play is supposed to be about a midsummer *night's* dream, this opening scene takes place by day. That is reassuring in a way: there can be something scary about the night and its dark shadows, and it is nice to be able to see everything clearly and know just what is what. At the same time, though, there is less scope for illusion in the 'cold light of day', and illusions can be sustaining. By night, in our dreams, we can be anything, anyone we want. Scary as it may be, in some ways the night can seem preferable.

The play begins with thoughts of love, Theseus looking forward to his marriage with Hippolyta. His eager anticipation comes through in verse (lines 3–4): *But O, methinks, how slow/This old moon wanes*. Read the lines aloud. Three consecutive stresses on *old moon wanes* slow line 4 down (line 3 skips along by comparison), conveying Theseus's impatience.

FATHER KNOWS BEST?

Egeus appears spouting his rights under the law, authority and duty. Suddenly, the mood of the scene becomes more serious. Theseus is not a lover any more but the Duke – the man in charge of laying down the law. If he has private desires, he also has public duties. So does Hermia, he says. She must choose between marriage with the man her father chooses, lifelong virginity in a convent, or death. ❂ What do you think she should do?

Egeus's view is clear. He wants Hermia to marry Demetrius. He tells Lysander (lines 97–8): *And she is mine, and all my right of her/I do estate unto Demetrius*. He talks about his daughter in legal language, as if she were a piece of land or property.

Left behind together, Lysander and Hermia talk, not of law and duty but of love and desire. But the contrast in language is not as strong as you might expect, for Hermia uses a legalistic language of her own. Where Egeus and Theseus talked of the laws of Athens, she speaks of *tale* and *history*. Look closely, though, and there is a lot in common between her language (lines 150–5) and the two men's:

> If then true lovers ever have been crossed
> It stands as an edict in destiny.
> Then let us teach our trial patience,
> Because it is a customary cross ...

LEGAL NICETIES

Words like *edict* and *trial* here are legalistic, while *customary* suggests the legal notion of 'precedent' – things have always been done this way before, so they should be done the same way now. Hermia is proposing a separate code of law specially for young people, following the precedents laid down by the old love stories and the great lovers of history. ✪ Look at the oath she takes (lines 169–75): normally we swear by God or by some sacred object like the Bible – what does it say about Hermia's state of mind that she is swearing by these particular things?

BEYOND THE LAW

If the law of Athens forbids their love, Hermia and Lysander decide, they will get out of the city to where the law cannot follow them. Helena appears, feeling that life is all very unfair. Demetrius's love for Hermia, she says, breaks the laws not just of Athens but of common sense. She, Helena, is just as beautiful as Hermia, so why should Demetrius not love her? But love is not logical like this, of course: it is a matter of perception.

Helena says she wishes she could be *translated* (line 191). She cannot be turned into Hermia, of course, but what she is saying may not be quite as absurd as it seems. Love does have the power to change things. Look at Hermia's own comment (lines 204–8) that for her Lysander has turned Athens from a paradise into a hell. Love isn't necessarily all sweet and nice.

BEYOND REASON

Love has certainly changed Helena, apparently robbing her of all reason. From the point of view of sheer calculation, it would be in her own interests to cover up for her friends' elopement. That way Hermia would be out of the picture, and Demetrius might feel he had to settle for Helena after all. Instead, for the hope of a few words of gratitude from Demetrius, she will risk not only her friendship with Hermia but her own chances of happiness. It makes no sense.

Love breaks the rules, then, and throws everything into a different light. Such a different light, indeed, that perhaps it is better suited to darkness, where the things of everyday life cannot be seen and the imagination can range free.

Lysander and Hermia have agreed to meet in the middle of a wood in the middle of the night. There, outside the city, away from the authority of parents and the law, they will find freedom. There, in the peace of the wood, as the night comes down and everyday realities dissolve into darkness, the lovers will be able to imagine their own new world. Anything is possible in the world of dream.

 ### SPOTLIGHT ON CHANGE

Think about the idea of change. We have seen how the feelings we have can change the way we look at things. As Helena says:

> *Things base and vile, holding no quantity,*
> *Love can transpose to form and dignity.*
> *Love looks not with the eyes, but with the mind*
> *And therefore is winged Cupid painted blind.*

But the feelings we have can themselves be changed by poetry, claims Egeus. Look at it from his point of view – a bit of moonlight, a bit of mood music and above all a bit of poetry, and his dutiful daughter Hermia has been changed into a teenage rebel:

> *Thou, thou, Lysander, thou hast given her rhymes,*
> *And interchanged love tokens with my child.*
> *Thou hast by moonlight at her window sung*
> *With feigning voice verses of feigning love …*
> *With cunning hast thou filched my daughter's heart …*

It may not be quite the sort of wizardry Egeus thinks it is, but words and settings really do have the power to change the way people feel. At its most benign, perhaps, this magic might be worked by a love poem like Lysander's. More disturbingly, perhaps, it might be a political speech. The person who has command over language may well end up having command over people.

Over to you

? The diagram below shows the command structure of the characters in this scene (who's supposed to obey who). Try tracing on top of this the love-lines (who wants who). Consider how the two diagrams compare. Can you see any accidents waiting to happen, any conflicts in store?

Theseus   Hippolyta

Egeus

Lysander   Demetrius   Helena   Hermia

? Courtship – what do we know about the courtship of (a) Theseus and Hippolyta (lines 116–17), and (b) Lysander and Hermia (lines 128–35)? Which lady seems to have more choice in the matter, and why?

? How does Helena characterise love in her speech at the end of the scene? To Egeus (line 128) love is a spell. Find three further definitions in the course of the scene.

? What sort of mood do you think Shakespeare creates in this opening scene? Is this to be a light, upbeat play or a dark, downbeat one?

? Divide a sheet of paper down the middle, head one side 'Up' and the other 'Down', then read through Theseus's opening speech noting down in the appropriate column any words which seem to you to suggest one mood or the other. Words that suggest joy, life, light or indeed anything positive will belong in the 'up' column, then, while words with darker, more negative associations will go under 'down'. Continue through the rest of the scene, and when you've finished, see how the two lists compare.

now you've seen the nobles, take a break before seeing how the other half live

Act 1 scene 2

◆ A group of Athenian tradesmen plan a performance for the royal wedding celebrations.
◆ They agree to meet the next night to rehearse in a wood outside the city.

The difference in mood in this scene is enormous – light comedy after the drama of the first. But the difference in social tone is perhaps even greater. If in scene 1 we met some of Athens' higher society, this scene introduces some of the city's working men. The difference is clear from the start: you get a strong message from the very names of these men: 'Snug', 'Snout', and of course 'Bottom' – comically short, simple, crudely English words next to the elaborate, elegant classical-sounding names of the last scene: 'Demetrius', 'Lysander', 'Hippolyta', and so on.

CLOTHES AND CLASS

The social difference would display itself in the men's costumes, of course, and in their gestures and their way of carrying themselves: the moment they entered the stage it would be clear that they came from a very different class than the aristocrats we have just been watching.

Once they open their mouths, the difference is even more obvious. We saw at the end of Act 1, scene 1 how the command of language could lead to the command of people. The opposite certainly seems to hold: lack of linguistic command tends to go along with powerlessness. For all their verbal energy, the inarticulacy of the workmen renders their low status unmistakable. To be inarticulate is, effectively, to lack a voice.

The tradesmen's lack of education is clearly comic, but they are not in the play just for us to laugh at. They also serve to send up the pretensions of the more upper-class characters. Bottom doesn't know the story of *Pyramus and Thisbe*, though it belongs to the classical mythology, so if he were more educated he would. Ignorant as he is, though, he has seen enough junk theatre to ask: *What is Pyramus? A lover or a tyrant?* He knows from experience that the lead male character in a play is likely to fall into one of those two categories. In scene 1 we admired Lysander's romantic eloquence and Theseus's regal authority. It does something to the way we regard them to be reminded now that the lover and the tyrant are 'stock' characters. Such standard, often-repeated and hence instantly familiar figures are a convenient short-cut for the busy commercial dramatist, slotting easily into an unfolding action without any need for careful character development.

The disadvantage of such characters is that they are too familiar, and too superficially conceived, to be either interesting as sketches of human nature or compelling as characters. There is more to both Theseus and Lysander than that, of course, but as readers/watchers we get a more critical take on them when we are reminded that there are conventions – even clichés – in these things. Neither is really a 'stock' character: but at the same time, perhaps, both are less special than they themselves like to think!

SPOTLIGHT ON THEATRE

❂ How do you think this group of characters would behave on the stage, *physically*? How would they move, place themselves? Think of a class of seven-year-olds, whose teacher is handing out the parts for the school Christmas play:

41

there is always one kid who has to be the star, others who shrink back from the prospect of performance – and since a part has to be found for everyone, you end up with somebody having to play the donkey or the fifth shepherd's dog!

Funny as this scene is, it has serious things to say about the play as a whole – even, perhaps, about theatre more generally. The tradesmen's failure to understand the conventions of theatre is obvious; considered more closely, that failure can be seen to spring from two separate misconceptions.

First there is the view of the stagestruck Bottom. He sees the play as an opportunity for self-exhibition – a vehicle for his own majestic (he imagines) talents. The thought that it might have a wider purpose, in representing a story, creating an illusion, doesn't occur to him.

Until, that is, he is shocked out of his self-regard by Quince: *And you should do it too terribly you would fright the Duchess and the ladies that they would shriek, and that were enough to hang us all*. And that is the second misconception: it is ridiculous, of course, to think that some pantomime lion is really going to frighten anyone. Quince is going to the other extreme and exaggerating the realism of the illusion.

That is the tricky thing about the theatre. We believe and we don't believe at the same time. If we are not prepared to let ourselves be fooled at all, we cannot respond to the situations and feelings being represented before us; but we never believe that what's happening on stage is literally 'true'.

There is magic in the theatre. A group of actors have already been transformed into Athenian aristocrats and workmen before our very eyes. It takes imagination, though: Shakespeare's, the actors', our own.

Try this

? Why do the workmen decide to rehearse their play in the wood?

? Who seems to be the leader of the workmen in this scene? Who is the biggest show-off of the company?

Who would you say was the most timid? Find something in the text to support your view in each case.

? This second scene features uneducated men who set out to say one thing and end up saying another. Look at how Quince (lines 6–7) seems stupidly to be contradicting himself (*wedding day at night*) when really, if you think about it for a moment, what he is saying makes perfect sense. It is just awkwardly expressed. Now go through the scene and write down all the words you can find which are misused. How do these mistakes affect what their speakers are trying to say?

take a break now – next stop fairyland!

Act 2 *scene* 1

◆ Puck, jester to the Fairy King Oberon, warns a fairy servant to Queen Titania of his master's rage over the Queen's 'theft' of a boy-companion.
◆ The royal couple meet and quarrel.
◆ Oberon plots revenge and sends Puck off for a magic herb. This will make the sleeping Titania fall in love with the first thing she sees on waking.
◆ Oberon sees a youth (Demetrius) being dogged by a desperate maiden (Helena). He sends Puck after them, so the magic can be worked on the unfeeling young man as well.

We are now well into the play, beginning the second act. It still feels fresh, though, since every scene so far has presented us with a change in pace and tone (the drop down the social ladder we saw between Act 1, scene 1 and Act 1, scene 2, for instance, and the switch from verse to prose that helped to signal it) and a new and completely different set of characters: the young nobles in Act 1, scene 1, the *mechanicals* in Act 1, scene 2. This scene, too, introduces a new set of characters, only this time they are not mortals, but spirits. Notice the

short-lined, rather formal verse these first fairy speakers use –
another thing we have not had before (unless you want to
count Bottom's 'lofty' rhyme at Act 1, scene 2, lines 26–33!).

NIGHT TIME IN THE WOOD

We are also in another setting, in the wood by night. This
difference is one you have to keep consciously in mind
when reading the play: in the theatre, of course, the very
different sort of lighting – dark, shadowy, mysterious –
you would have for this scene would make it
unmissable. Now we really are in the world of dream, of
fantasy. The fairy's opening speech suggests a world in which
the ordinary human rules do not apply. What would be
obstacles to us – *bush … briar … flood … fire* – cannot
impede this spirit. *Swifter than the moon's sphere*, she travels:
the comparison suggests not only speed, but vast, astronomical
distances, effortlessly covered.

Everything is extravagantly transformed in this
dreamland: the flowers become *pensioners* – a royal
bodyguard, laden with rich jewellery. But this image, for all its
dazzling beauty, also carries a hint of menace. The Queen's
guards are, after all, armed soldiers sworn to kill or die in her
defence.

THE WILD SIDE

And she might need them to. Look at Puck's speech (lines
18–31). The King may be here to hold *revels*, but he is none
the less *passing fell and wrath*, and *jealous*. And while the
Queen may pamper and caress her *lovely boy, so sweet a
changeling*, with *joy*, there is a suggestion of violence, too,
about the fact that she has *stol'n* him, and now *perforce
withholds* him. The elves have to *hide* for *fear*, we are told.
There is a world of pleasure and enchantment in the wood: but
there are hints too of something more threatening. Groves,
greens and fountains sound enticing enough – but what about
forests wild (line 25)?

A MATTER OF SCALE

Notice that, in addition to all the other differences in tone and setting we mentioned above, there is a difference in scale. The Queen has little flowers for guardsmen, we have already been told, while the frightened elves hide in *acorn cups* (lines 30–1). It is not just a *difference* in scale, though, but a confusion: as we saw in the fairy's opening speech, these tiny spirits take vast distances in their stride, while the Queen, we are told, has as a companion, a boy – apparently a human-scale boy from a mortal Indian king. It is hard for us to make sense of these apparent contradictions, but then it is hard to make sense of fairydom altogether: that is the whole point. How, for instance, are we going to pin down Puck when, as the fairy has told us (line 40), he has at least two other distinct identities, as *Hobgoblin* and *Robin Goodfellow*?

Indeed both the fairy's remarks about Puck (lines 34–42) – and Puck's own proud boasts after that (lines 42–57) – suggest that upsetting the normal human routines and ways of understanding things is a large part of what fairydom's activities are about. We see the same when Oberon accuses Titania of manipulating Theseus's behaviour for her own ends (lines 77–80):

> *Didst thou not lead him through the glimmering night*
> *From Perigouna whom he ravishèd,*
> *And make him with fair Aigles break his faith,*
> *With Ariadne and Antiopa?*

These represent direct and damaging interventions by the Fairy Queen in the lives of innocent mortal women.

A ROYAL ROW

And as Theseus and Hippolyta prepare for their wedding, it is sobering to find fairyland's royal marriage on the rocks. But then the spirit realm is, it seems, anything but idealistic. With all the magic powers at his command, there is something sadistic about Puck's love of practical jokes. As for Oberon and Titania, far from being particularly spiritual and regal, it is funny that they are in some ways the most 'human' couple in the play: they squabble like any mortal couple (lines 60–8).

Titania's speech (lines 81–117) develops further the association of love with disruption and violence, and gives still greater emphasis to the parallel between dreamworld and reality. The falling out of the fairy King and Queen has had disastrous consequences for the mortal world, she says. Their love has always made that world go round: so now, she says, their quarrels have left everything out of joint, even the seasons – the most important rhythm of human life.

Oberon's story about Cupid and his dart adds yet another example of the violent, predatory nature love can often assume, and the way in which it can upset the normal order of things. But the magical properties Cupid's arrow left the plant with remind us of another property of love. Squeezed on a person's eye, the magic juice alters their perception of things completely. In that respect, it can stand for love itself: as we said in our discussion of Act 1, scene 1, above, love has the capacity to change the way we see.

POINTS OF VIEW

For the moment, though, Demetrius and Helena see things very differently. Demetrius cannot see why she is unable to see the obvious: he simply does not love her. It is no use his explaining, and the result is confusion – and transformation, for the desperate Helena willingly imagines herself changed into his *spaniel* (line 203). Her situation, she feels, changes 'the story' itself:

> *Apollo flies, and Daphne holds the chase.*
> *The dove pursues the griffin; the mild hind*
> *Makes speed to catch the tiger: bootless speed,*
> *When cowardice pursues, and valour flies.*
> (lines 231–4)

The confusion Helena describes is comparable to the disorder described by Titania earlier. But Helena's hunting image has associations of violence and destruction too. For all the terrible natural disasters described earlier in the scene, the mood has not really started to darken till now: Demetrius's warning (lines

214–19) has already soured the mood, and his ungallant threat to leave Helena to the wild beasts does nothing to improve matters. He really excels himself in lines 236–7, however, which sound unpleasantly like a threat of rape. ✪ Do you think he means it, or is he just trying to get rid of her?

 The arrival of Demetrius and Helena is the first example of what will be an important theme in the play: that of eavesdropping, of spectating and surveillance. In a sense the whole experience of theatre-going is like this. *A Midsummer Night's Dream* makes a feature of it, though: the audience in the theatre often being matched by another audience actually on the stage. This sort of situation naturally produces **dramatic ironies**: moments when the audience knows more than the characters it is watching. Like Oberon, for instance, we see Demetrius's situation more clearly than he does himself. He is *meant* for Helena, we know: that is the way the story has to go. Oberon's silent vow that: *Ere he do leave this grove/ Thou shalt flie him, and he shall seek thy love* is a promise to restore *the story to* its rightful order. In the meantime, he will be taking rather more malicious steps to change the way his queen sees the world.

STYLE AND LANGUAGE

The bank Titania sometimes sleeps on (lines 249–56) sounds a beautiful place – think of all the different senses this passage appeals to. Sight, certainly, and smell ... but what about the sound of the words? Some of these (*oxlips ... luscious ... sweet musk-roses ...*) are curiously sensuous too, and even the sheer number of different flowers, named one after the other like this, seems to suggest the rich luxury of Titania's bed.

In such a warm, soft setting the snake seems a chilling, sinister presence. What is it doing here? Well, reflecting Oberon's ill will, obviously, for one thing. Given that it has just cast its skin, though, it also represents change – the possibility of change for the better, the fear of change for the worse.

SPOTLIGHT ON SPELLS

We considered at the start of this scene how the fairy world is
a place of jewels, flowers and other beautiful things. We saw
it then in terms of change, fairy magic turning dew into
jewellery and an ordinary bank of cowslips into a royal
guard. There is more to it than this, though.

The scene seems to say that if you can look at the world
with a sufficiently imaginative eye, you too may see in
everyday reality something beautiful, something enchanted.

Much of the beauty in Fairyland resides in the small things,
the details – in the little spots on a cowslip flower, the drops
of dew, the *spangled starlight sheen* and *acorn cups*. If we
have not seen these things, this magic, maybe we just haven't
been looking hard enough.

The magic of perception is the magic of poetry too. Seen this
way, an image is the equivalent of a spell. Shakespeare's
fairyland represents as literal fact what happens all the time in
writing – but as imagery. A **metaphor** can be seen as a sort of
spell: the poet who sees a flower as a soldier is in some sense
turning it into one; the writer who says a dewdrop is like a
jewel is making the same sort of transformation.

Over to you

? Titania's speech in lines 81–117 describes all manner
of natural disaster – *murrion*, or sheep disease, for
instance. What others can you find?

? The emotional tangles of Fairyland can lead to human
misery, we have seen. What is the source of the
current conflict between Oberon and Titania?

? In lines 195–7 Helena compares Demetrius's heart to
adamant – magnetised metal. What two properties of
adamant does she see in Demetrius? Talking about
herself, she also uses images of metal: *iron* and *steel*:
what do you think these words say about Helena and
her love?

? In lines 155–74, Oberon describes how Cupid's arrow fell on a flower. How did it change that flower's appearance? And how did it change its properties: what magical powers did it give the flower?

? Just about everybody who *is* anybody in this scene is either watching or following somebody else. Below is a list of the main characters in this scene. Join the names up in sequence to show who's watching/following whom. Start with the audience, ourselves. After all, we're watching everybody else:

Audience

Helena

Oberon

Hermia and Lysander

Demetrius

if you want to stay more alert than Titania does in the next scene, take a break

---

Act 2 *scene* 2

◆ The fairies sing to Titania.
◆ As Titania sleeps, Oberon squeezes juice from the herb onto her eye.
◆ Lysander and Hermia arrive, lost and exhausted. They bed down to sleep till daylight, lying chastely apart, as they are still unmarried.
◆ Puck mistakes them for the couple his master sent him after, and treats Lysander with the herb.
◆ Helena arrives, Demetrius having finally managed to shake off her pursuit,
◆ She wakes Lysander, who promptly falls for her.
◆ Helena assumes it's a sick joke, and runs off, but lovesick Lysander follows.
◆ Hermia wakes up abandoned and alone.

For all the magic charms the fairy song is supposed to contain, it casts its most effective spell not as a piece of supernatural sorcery but as more earthly, artistic enchantment – as a soothing lullaby, which sends Titania to sleep in seconds. The everyday magic of music casts the strongest spell of all! The combined effects of melody and harmony, the regular rhythms of the fairies' verses, and the stately spectacle of the dance are so strong that the song casts a soothing spell over Titania – even though the tone of its lyrics is actually anything but calming, raising ideas of creepy-crawlies, even poisonous snakes. So if Titania is soothed, we as the audience are not. We sense that the sinister side of Oberon's *I know a bank …* speech (Act 2, scene 1, lines 249–56) is echoed in the song's words, even if its rhythms and music recall the more pleasurable side of Oberon's speech.

HELENA'S TRANSFORMATIONS

Helena feels Demetrius's rejection has transformed her: she is *as ugly as a bear*, she says (line 100); her love's rejection has in some sense turned her into a *monster* (line 103) from whom *beasts* flee (line 101). Moments later, though, she undergoes a second ironic transformation. Remember Helena's wish (Act 1, scene 1, line 191) to be *translated* into Hermia? Well with Hermia's supposed love Lysander suddenly in love with her instead, it is rather as if she had been!

ALL TALK

Lysander in his poetic mode can sometimes seem too eloquent by half. It is not his fault, of course – he has been bewitched – but there is something disturbing none the less in the way Lysander can declare his passionate poetic love to two different girls in as many minutes. The language of love is supposed to be the most intimate, heartfelt sort of speech. Ironically, though, we find that the same words do just as well whatever woman is being wooed. ✪ How likeable a character do you now find Lysander?

Hermia is left alone in the wood. Within this dreamworld, she has had a dream of her own, and it has not been a pleasant one. The serpent mentioned in Oberon's *I know a bank …* speech and the fairies' song at the start of this scene (also, perhaps, the monster Helena thought she herself was turning into) has finally turned up in this horrible form. The *knight* (line 150) who should be saving this damsel in distress has instead sworn his allegiance to Helena. There is a real sense of shock and violence about Hermia's speech: *Help me, Lysander, help me!* You can almost feel the *crawling serpent* at her breast, feel her *quake* with fear, see her *swoon*. The attack may be a figment of her imagination, but her response to it is vividly physical.

Your turn

? Why does the magic juice have to be applied to Titania's eyes, rather than any other place?

? How do Lysander and Hermia come to be lying apart from one another? And how does Puck manage to mistake them for Demetrius and Helena?

? Look back at the diagram you did at the end of Act 1, scene 1, p. 39, showing the characters and their love-lines. How do things look now? Draw in the new lines in a different colour if you want.

next we see that love really is blind – but first, take a break

Act 3 *scene* 1

◆ The tradesmen have gathered in the wood to rehearse their play.

◆ Puck gives Bottom the Weaver an ass's head and the others flee in alarm.

◆ Titania wakes up, sees Bottom and falls instantly in love.

Once again the workmen ludicrously overestimate the likely realism of their play. Unfamiliar themselves with the conventions of theatre, they assume that others will take their acting for reality, and so they devise elaborate strategies for making their play acceptable by undermining its dramatic impact. They fail to understand, too, that there is no need to have actors playing inanimate objects like the moon and the wall. Flute, in line 87 onwards, will run his whole part together without waiting for the other characters to speak. All in all, in showing how a play *should not* be staged, this scene does a pretty good job of making us think what a remarkable thing a successful theatrical performance really is.

 From line 77, we get our first look at the actual words of the tradesmen's play. Shakespeare may be having fun at the expense of lesser talents than his own, but he is also making a more serious point about poetry and its capacity to shape the way we look at things.

If good poetry can seduce us, bad poetry can put us off. A tale of two lovers, separated by a wall and by the enmity of their families, it is easy to imagine the story of *Pyramus and Thisbe* being a moving romantic drama, even if here it is quite the reverse. Comedy or tragedy: it's the way you tell 'em!

STYLE AND LANGUAGE

✪ So what do you think of the way the author of *Pyramus and Thisbe* tells it? He is not helped by his actors, of course. Confusing *odorous* with *odious*, and telling Flute that Pyramus has gone off to *see a noise*, Bottom makes clear just how far he is out of his depth intellectually. But even without his ignorant mistakes, how accomplished a piece of writing do you think this is? Pyramus, for example, is *lily white* and *red rose* in consecutive lines. Leaving aside the contradiction, how original do you think these images are?

Thisbe's comparison of her love with a true, tireless horse is picked up comically when Bottom appears with the head of an ass. Puck's speech (*Sometimes a horse I'll be, sometime a hound ...*) underlines this idea of transformation, while adding a further note of menace to the proceedings. As we found before, in Act 2, scene 1, there can be a vicious quality to Puck's practical jokes, and this threat to harass Bottom's friends in a series of animal forms shows real aggression – towards men who have, after all, done him no harm. In fact Bottom is the one who harries them, albeit unintentionally, when he re-enters with his ass's head and they scatter in panic. Their fear and flight at his appearance are especially funny given the fuss they made earlier about how their stage lion might frighten the ladies (lines 25–30).

MAKING AN ASS OF BOTTOM

As Quince now points out, Bottom has been *translated.* This is the same word Helena used (Act 1, scene 1, line 191), and it echoes her later feeling (Act 2, scene 2, lines 100, 103) that she had been turned into an ugly animal. Though Bottom does not understand what has happened to him, he comes comically close without realising it when he says *This is to make an ass of me* – though he obviously only means it in the sense of 'making a fool of'. Oberon, remember (Act 2, scene 2, lines 36–40), wanted Titania to wake to love some ferocious animal. By making Titania fall in love with the ass-headed Bottom, Puck is going one better. Titania's loving a fierce animal would just be dangerous and inappropriate; her loving Bottom in this form will be ridiculous and humiliating. In making an ass of Bottom, Puck is making an ass of her.

ASS OR ANGEL?

Titania is woken by Bottom's singing (his braying voice as different as can be imagined from those of the birds he is singing about!). She thinks he sounds like an angel (line 122); but then she also thinks he is *as wise as* [he is] *beautiful* (line 140)! She is under the spell of Oberon's herb, of course.

Notice that, while the Queen speaks in verse here – verse which catches in its rhythms the gentle, romantic mood of fairyland and love – Bottom speaks in his usual rambling prose.

Added to this, Bottom's perceptions are basic and matter-of-fact, and Titania's exaggeratedly romantic. It is as if they are taking part in different scenes. Titania offers a dreamy existence of *jewels* and *flowers* that recalls the fairy's description of fairyland at the beginning of Act 2, scene 1, and Oberon's *I know a bank* ... speech at the end of that scene. Bottom, however, is speaking crude common sense, and the contrast is comic.

Another comic contrast comes with the arrival of the fairies. From their very names they seem tiny and insubstantial beside Bottom's lumbering bulk. Look at Titania's instructions to them for Bottom's care (*Be kind and courteous to this gentleman ...*). The fairies' lightness and tiny size is repeatedly emphasised.

The scene ends with a grotesque sting in the tail, in Titania's closing remark that her minions should *Tie up my love's tongue; bring him silently*. Bottom's braying conversation is, it seems, making the illusion of his beauty and gentility difficult to maintain, even for Titania in her bewitched state!

SPOTLIGHT ON BOTTOM

Part of the humour in Titania's courtship of Bottom, we have seen, stems from the difference between Titania's attitude of romanticism and Bottom's crude common sense. Another comic aspect, we found, was the ludicrous difference in size between Bottom and his attendants. But the situation is also absurd from the point of view of sex-roles and social class as Shakespeare's audience would have seen them. We saw when we looked at Act 2, scene 1 that it flies in the face of convention – changes *the story*, as Helena put it then – that the lady should be wooing the gentleman. But it changes the story even more outrageously when, as here, the lady is a queen and the man a common weaver.

Likeably enough, Bottom doesn't know how to behave in the grand role bestowed on him by the Queen. He chats pleasantly and on equal terms with the fairies appointed to serve him. Charming as this may be, it would have seemed grossly comic to the play's original audience, marking a preposterous collapse of authority, an absurd up-ending of the normal social order.

Got the picture

? The workmen decide they must reassure the female members of their audience on two points. Can you say what they are?

? They also discuss two more technical challenges: things they feel will be hard to represent on stage. What are these, and how do they decide to get round them?

? Pyramus and Thisbe are supposed to meet by moonlight. Which other couples in the play have met by moonlight?

? From their very names, as we said above, the fairies called by Titania (line 153) to look after Bottom seem tiny and insubstantial. Now look at Titania's more detailed instructions to them in lines 155–65: write down the words and phrases in this speech which suggest the fairies' airy lightness and miniature scale.

now you've got to the Bottom of this scene, take a break

Act 3 *scene* 2

◆ Puck tells Oberon he has carried out his order, but it becomes apparent that he has treated the wrong couple.

◆ When Demetrius lies down to sleep, Puck has a second chance to get things right.

◆ This time, Helena arrives. Already being pestered by Lysander, she now finds Demetrius declaring his love as well.

◆ Hermia returns, accusing her of stealing Lysander's love, and Helena concludes that her former friends have ganged up to taunt her.

◆ As the girls quarrel, the men go off to fight a duel over Helena.

◆ Oberon tells Puck to lead the lovers off through the wood till each has been matched with his/her right partner.

This scene features three ill-matched couples: first Titania and Bottom, as described by Puck to his master Oberon; second Hermia and Demetrius; third Helena and Lysander.

 ### STYLE AND LANGUAGE

↷ Notice that, just as Puck's magic has given Bottom an ass's head, his words now give animal form to the other mechanicals: they scattered, he says (lines 20–1), like *geese* spotting a wildfowler or *choughs* (jackdaws) hearing a gun.

♥ In his wooing of Hermia, from line 43 onwards, Demetrius is using the same language of love we have seen Lysander use. It is wildly inappropriate, not only on account of Hermia's negative feelings towards Demetrius (to whom, remember, her father has been trying to marry her

55

against her will) but because of the real distress she's in following her nightmare and abandonment. She fears Lysander is literally dead. But Demetrius has a lover's easy way with words. When Hermia accuses him of murder, he replies that she is murdering him by breaking his heart (lines 59–60). Hence Hermia's exasperated exclamation (line 68): *O, once tell true, tell true*. All this high-flown, riddling language has left her dizzy: she is desperate for some plain speaking, for someone to tell her genuinely and simply what has happened to someone she genuinely and simply cares about.

The unscrupulousness of love and its language are again highlighted when Lysander offers to *yield* Demetrius his *part* in Hermia, if Demetrius *bequeaths* him his share of Helena's love. Love is now speaking the same language of law and property that Egeus was speaking in Act 1, scene 1. Demetrius, too, makes poetic language work for him, saying (lines 171–2) that his heart went to Hermia only as a guest, and that Helena is its true home. The merest play on words, this 'argument' still seems to satisfy him.

A FRIENDSHIP ON THE ROCKS?

Believing that her friend has joined with the others to make a fool of her (line 192), Helena recalls the long friendship that once joined her to Hermia. The separation of two such friends (*Two lovely berries moulded on one stem,/... two seeming bodies but one heart*) involves real violence; the distress Helena feels when her wish to be *translated* into her friend is granted, and the shock that results for Hermia herself, illustrate again the darker potential of love. Helena's speech also highlights the damage that the violent passions of love can do to what are in many ways more real, lasting relationships, like her lifelong friendship with Hermia. We saw at the end of Act 1, scene 1 how the lovesick Helena was prepared to betray her friend's elopement for a word of gratitude from Demetrius. Now the women's apparent rivalry in love is poisoning their whole friendship. ❂ How do you rate the relative value of love and friendship? How do you think Shakespeare sees them?

The situation degenerates into farce, Lysander shaking off Hermia's embrace and (lines 260–1) calling her *cat* ...

serpent (the last is especially unkind, given the monstrous snake which attacked her in her recent dream). Now it is Hermia's turn to be transformed into an animal. Comparing her to a 'burr', a sticking plant-head, places her even lower down the evolutionary scale so is perhaps still more insulting. Ridiculous though it may be, this attack still leaves a bad taste. Bewitched as he is, Lysander doesn't merely prefer Helena, he feels a physical revulsion towards Hermia. She has become something *vile*.

The girls, hitherto inseparable friends, are now brawling. Such a violent falling out between two such ladylike characters is a shocking spectacle. There is humour, of course, in hearing Helena deliver a view of Hermia she has apparently revised since her all-but-sisters speech earlier (lines 202–14). Now she recalls that Hermia *was a vixen when she went to school* (line 325).

 STYLE AND LANGUAGE

There is humour too in seeing how the language the girls use in describing one another – especially on the subject of height – squares with the descriptions we have been given of them by their poetic male admirers. Demetrius, says Helena (lines 226–7), has just described her as *goddess, nymph, divine, and rare,/ Precious, celestial.* Now (line 296) Hermia calls her a *painted maypole.* Hermia's unflattering description underlines the exaggeration in Demetrius's.

Notice, too, that the height question, a running joke through the rest of the scene, is only introduced because Hermia misinterprets a comment of Helena's. Her word *puppet* (line 288) is obviously intended as an attack on Hermia's integrity, reinforcing the preceding charge that she is a *counterfeit* – a fake, a pretend person. Hermia, however, immediately thinks it's a reference to her size. This is a nice human touch: we are so used to hearing Hermia described in Lysander and Demetrius's high-flown terms, that it is a surprise to find that this model of poetic perfection is an ordinary young woman who is touchy about her height!

THE DARKEST HOUR

But for all the humour, this is the play's bleakest phase by far. By now what we have is a Midsummer Night's Nightmare. We have already talked about the dark, ruthless side of love and the slippery, sinister side to poetic language. We have also seen – especially in Puck's sadistic streak – a less appealing side to the powers of magic and fairyland. All seems to have come together here to leave a desperate, irredeemable mess.

But if this is the play's bleakest moment, a moment, thankfully, is all it is. Oberon's anger with Puck brings us an immediate sense of relief. Normally anger is a negative emotion: here, though, it is our guarantee that Oberon's intentions are basically good, that he is committed to bringing things to a happy conclusion.

The first thing to be done, says Oberon, is that Demetrius and Lysander – who have gone off into the wood to fight a duel over who is to have Helena – must be separated. The *drooping fog* (line 357) in which they are to lose themselves will, paradoxically, redouble the darkness of night and take them through darkness and confusion to the light, clarity and understanding of day. In a single line, then, we find a hint as to the possible purpose of the play as a whole – a journey through darkness, suffering and confusion to a better, more enlightened existence. The fact that the fog is to be *as black as Acheron* – one of the rivers of Hades, the Underworld to which the dead made their way in the myths of classical Greece – suggests that this journey can even be seen as a sort of death and rebirth. All of which makes an outwardly light comedy suddenly seem like a very serious drama indeed!

A NARROW ESCAPE

Puck's speech about the approaching dawn (*My fairy lord, this must be done with haste ...*, lines 378–87), also hints at a much darker side to the supernatural than has mostly been acknowledged so far. In the account of fairyland at the beginning of Act 2, scene 1, for instance, or the world

Titania offers Bottom in Act 3, scene 1, line 147 onwards, Fairyland is associated with gentleness, luxury, light, happiness and abundance. We have already had inklings at various points that this is not all there is to it. But Puck's description here is far and away the most chilling we have had. Think what it would have done to the tone of the scene if it had come before Oberon's words of reassurance! Coming after, it still sends a bit of a shudder down the spine. We feel we have had a narrow escape from forces much too dark for comfort.

But Oberon again (lines 354–78) disassociates himself from this sort of supernatural existence. He is the sort of spirit who can stay up into the dawn, he says, meaning that, though on occasion mischievous, he is basically benevolent. His urgings to Puck to *make no delay;/ We may effect this business yet ere day* (lines 394–5) suggest that the action has passed its crisis. All that remains is to sort out the confusions and tie up the loose ends.

Puck's song (lines 396–9) and his actions in leading the two would-be duellists astray echo his gloating words in Act 3, scene 1, lines 101–6 (*I'll follow you, I'll lead you about a round …*) and his cruel harrying of the mechanicals once Bottom has been transformed. This time, though, the action is kindly – another sign that what has been wrong in the night's activities is now to be put right.

The whole unhappy mess, says Puck, when Hermia appears in a state, indicates that:

> *Cupid is a knavish lad*
> *Thus to make poor females mad.*

This is a bit much, given his own contribution to the upset and confusion! But now, he says, anointing Lysander's eye to restore his love for Hermia, everything is going to turn out right:

> *Jack shall have Jill,*
> *Naught shall go ill,*
> *The man shall have his mare again,*
> *And all shall be well.*

STYLE AND LANGUAGE

The simple names and homely, nursery-rhyme form of this little verse show up the elaborate artificiality of the sort of poetic love-language we saw the aristocratic young lovers using earlier in the scene. It makes a bit of a joke of love, making something blunt and yokelish of an emotion which has previously been described in rather grander, more high-flown terms – but there is no harm in that. We have seen throughout that the elaborately poetic terms in which Lysander in particular has described love can be misleading and unreliable. We have seen, too, that love can be a violent, changeable and disruptive thing. It is important, then, to remember that it is also a basic fact of human existence. That is what Puck's words remind us of, in their homespun, even vulgar simplicity: in all times, at every level of society, young men and women have paired off into loving couples.

Test yourself

? In the quarrel between Helena and Hermia in this scene, the former's height and the latter's shortness become a sort of running gag, with even Lysander joining in eventually. Look through the scene again from line 288 to line 344 and note down the different words and phrases in which the idea recurs.

? Look closely at Puck's speech (lines 378–87). What sort of picture of the supernatural world does it present? Which words and phrases help give this impression? Now look back at the fairy's speech in Act 2, scene 1, lines 6–15, and see how the language of the two speeches compares.

now that a happy ending is in sight, take a break

Act 4 *scene* 1

◆ Oberon releases Titania from her spell and they are reconciled.

◆ He gives Bottom his own head back, and leaves him sleeping.

◆ Theseus, Hippolyta and Egeus arrive for a dawn hunt. They find the young people sleeping, now perfectly matched in love: Demetrius with Helena, and Lysander with Hermia.

◆ Egeus is angry, but Demetrius says he is happy with the way things have turned out. Theseus rules that the lovers should all be married at the same ceremony as himself and Hippolyta.

◆ Bottom wakes up, astonished, and rushes off to tell the story of his amazing dream.

As we saw at the end of the last scene, the real drama is over. Now Oberon has undertaken to bring things out all right, we are in no real doubt as to the eventual outcome. But if the action is as good as over, what are the next two acts of the play supposed to be for? Some sense must be made of what has happened, for both characters and for audience. Not necessarily rational 'common' sense, but emotional, poetic sense. That is what the last two acts will be about.

TITANIA'S LOVE NEST

The scene opens in an atmosphere of obvious eroticism, with Titania's invitation to Bottom to sit down with her on a *flow'ry bed* (line 1), while she heaps caresses upon him. But it is hard to take such a seductive mood seriously, given Titania's references (lines 2–4) to her lover's *amiable cheeks*, his *sleek smooth head* and *fair large ears*! ✪ How do you think the actors playing Titania and Bottom should play this scene?

✪ As in Act 3, scene 1, there are absurdities of scale here: how far do you think one sac's worth of honey would go for a full-grown man? And it is hard to imagine a man like Bottom having such delicate appetites. Look what happens when the Queen calls for music: somehow, you can't help thinking that *the tongs and the bones* (lines 28–9) probably were not on the whole what she had in mind! Once again, as we saw earlier, at the end of Act 3, scene 1, Bottom's crudeness contrasts with the delicacy and refinement of Fairyland.

There is lots of humour here about Bottom's peculiar state, in between humanity and asshood, the man being surprised to find his face so *marvellous hairy* (line 24) but the ass in him craving oats, hay and dried peas (lines 31–2, 36). The main contrast, though, is that between the heavy grossness of humanity in general and the lightness and sophistication of fairydom. Hence, the squirrel's nuts Titania offers Bottom sound like fairy fare, found in the wood itself. The things he is asking for, on the other hand, sound like something from down on the farm. But Titania returns to the woods for the images she uses to suggest their embrace (lines 39–43):

> *So doth the woodbine the sweet honeysuckle*
> *Gently entwist; the female ivy so*
> *Enrings the barky fingers of the elm.*

Notice how the subject-word *woodbine* and its verb *entwist* are placed either side of the object-word *honeysuckle*, as if it really is 'entwisting' it!

HAS OBERON'S TRICK BACKFIRED?

It is no wonder, then, that Oberon should find the scene disagreeable when he comes upon it. We may find it charming, albeit comic: to him it is neither. His view of Bottom (line 48) as a *hateful fool* seems unjust, given the weaver's complete innocence in this whole affair and the part the King himself played in bringing it about. Could he be a little jealous, seeing his wife like this – even of the ass-headed Bottom? This was all Oberon's own doing, of course, his big scheme to punish and humiliate Titania, but he is the one who has ended up feeling punished and humiliated to see his wife in bed with an ass.

The ups and downs of human affairs are, we were told earlier in Titania's big speech at Act 2, scene 1, lines 81–117, influenced by the changing moods of the immortals. Now Oberon's softening attitude towards Titania signals a coming restoration of normality in the human world.

STYLE AND LANGUAGE

By line 62 Oberon is using the word *hateful* to describe the *imperfection* caused to Titania's eyes by the magic juice he placed in them. When this speech began, he was applying the word *hateful* to Bottom. The drift of this adjective from the one object to the other is revealing, reflecting as it does Oberon's movement from an irrationally angry blaming of the innocent Bottom to a realisation that what has happened has been the result of his own foolish trick.

Oberon calls Titania *my queen* again (line 84) when he invites her to dance with him. Their dance seals their reconciliation and anticipates the dancing there will be at Theseus's and Hippolyta's wedding feast the following night, at which the temporary confusions of the play's mortal lovers will be resolved in marriage.

As in Act 2, scene 2, music accompanies the working of magic: again, it has access to feelings that words cannot reach. The regular rhythms of these short, mostly rhymed lines (92–101) emphasise the tidy stability of the emotional order now prevailing in the play.

The idea of music then links this section with the following, the arrival of the royal hunting party being heralded by the sounds of horns, and Theseus commenting in line 105 upon the *music* of his hounds. In fact, the word *music* at this point stands for something rather different, suggesting not order and stability but profound disorientation. The *musical confusion/ Of hounds and echo in conjunction* (lines 109–10) resembles the crazy chaos of the soundtrack in a modern science-fiction or fantasy film at the moment where the action crosses a border of time, space or some other dimension and we move with the characters from one state of reality to another. Hippolyta's recollection of her hunt with Heracles and Cadmus has the same effect:

> *Never did I hear*
> *Such gallant chiding; for besides the groves,*
> *The skies, the fountains, every region near*
> *Seemed all one mutual cry.*

The whole scene seems to dissolve into sound here, heralding the lovers' emergence from their magic sleep.

The huntsmen's horns sound, and the lovers are suddenly back in the daytime world. Though geographically we are still in the wood, in the realm of magic and of night, we are effectively back in everyday Athens, where Theseus, not Oberon, is ruler.

Athenian law holds here, and under that law Egeus has rights over Hermia and over Lysander, who in legal terms is her abductor. But Demetrius disagrees and, under the law, Theseus, as Duke, can overrule Egeus, and, the law of romance, coinciding with the good of Athens, may be allowed to prevail.

Left behind by the departing hunting party, the lovers are left wondering what has happened to them. Hermia's sense is that she is seeing things *with parted eye,/ When everything seems double*. The idea recalls the theme of perception which has played such an important part in the play. How you see things determines how they are: hence with her eye treated with the magic herb, Titania was able to see Bottom with the ass's head and find him beautiful. Hermia here is seeing double, which is appropriate enough really: right now she has a foot in both worlds, she feels, the magical nightworld and the cold light of day, and she cannot be sure which of the two actually represents reality. As Demetrius puts it:

> *It seems to me*
> *That yet we sleep, we dream. Do not you think*
> *The Duke was here, and bade us follow him?*

– he is talking about Theseus's appearance, as if *he*, the solid, buinesslike Duke of Athens, were a dreamy, insubstantial spirit. It takes Demetrius and his friends several moments to decide that: *Why then, we are awake …*

COMPARING NOTES

Demetrius' parting remark that *by the way we shall recount our dreams* (line 197) reminds us that, though for the audience it has been a collective entertainment, Demetrius, Lysander, Hermia and Helena have each experienced the night's marvels individually and in a certain sense alone. They did not actually share the same experience, hence the need now to fill one another in. They have to work over the night's events and try to establish what has happened because, while each has been caught up in his or her own personalised 'dream', each has woken up in some significant sense changed by what has happened.

Demetrius's dream has ended in his ardently wooing the girl he earlier spurned, while Lysander, after for a time vehemently spurning the girl he loved, now has the official permission to marry her he never thought he would get; Hermia was abandoned for a time in the heart of the wood, while Helena, who had to tag along behind the rest, unwanted by anyone, before her strange if temporary transformation into everybody's love, now finds herself, after this strangest of nights, with the one love she really wanted all along. What has happened, while less solid than reality, has clearly been more substantial than a dream. If it is a dream, it is a dream whose effects have persisted past waking.

HOME TO ATHENS

As we said at the start of Act 1, scene 1, the daytime world is the only one we are really at home in: we cannot live permanently in the world of dream, enticing as that might (in some ways!) seem. But while it is important for the young lovers that they now return to daytime Athens, we none the less feel that, without their night of difficulties, they would have missed out on something important. The things they have seen and felt may have been figments of the imagination, but their legacy has been real enough; the bonds the lovers have formed as a result of their night in the wood are now unbreakable; their everyday Athenian reality has been touched by beauty, by enchantment.

This of course is one of the things art can do for us, one of the things which we may bring away from our experience of *A Midsummer Night's Dream*. Viewed at face value, the play is the merest fiction, a dressing-up game for grown-ups who ought to know better: somehow we sense, though, that it is something more than that. Unreal, insubstantial but by no means untrue or empty, the experience of a theatrical performance has a very tangible effect on our lives, the imaginary influencing our reality. That feeling of wonder, of magic, of the extraordinary which we find not only in plays but in music, books, films and other works of the imagination, enhances our appreciation of the ordinary here and now.

Test your recall

?   The loving togetherness of Titania and Bottom in the first part of this scene obviously annoys Oberon. What words and phrases show his displeasure, in lines 45–69?

?   Demetrius's final choice of a love has been altered by his experiences in the wood. In trying to explain this change of heart from line 159 onwards he uses a couple of images of natural transformation. Can you find them in the text?

?   What are Theseus's plans for the four young lovers as he leads them out of the wood (lines 176–85)?

?   There have been many references to music in this scene, especially (lines 102–39) the idea that the sounds made by a pack of hunting dogs is itself a kind of music. Look back at this section and see if you can find words in the text which suggest what kind of music this is.

now take a break before the wedding preparations begin

Act 4 *scene 2*

◆ The mechanicals are upset at Bottom's transformation – and the failure of their play.

◆ Bottom arrives, safe and sound: he has wonders to reveal, he says, but it will have to wait, since their play has been chosen for performance at the Royal Wedding celebrations.

Most obvious here is the difference in perspective between the working people of Athens and the play's more aristocratic characters. His friends' admiration and affection for Bottom is clear, but as poor men they cannot help feeling the financial loss involved in his disappearance. As Snug says, *If our sport had gone forward we had all been made men* – 'made' in the sense of being made, set up, for life. The difference in perspective is further underlined by Snug's mention of the *two or three lords and ladies more* to be married: it comes as a bit of a shock to us, having become so involved in the stories of Lysander and Hermia and Demetrius and Helena, but to Athens' lower classes they are of course very distant, anonymous figures.

Bottom's advice to his friends about their performance is, once again, amusingly literal-minded. Thisbe must have clean linen, and the lion not cut his fingernails – or what will he do for claws? Most of all, however, the actors must keep their breath free from onion or garlic. That way it will be sweet, and if their breath is sweet, he concludes – with crazy logic – their comedy will be too.

THREE WORLDS

As an audience, or as readers, we have seen the different characters in the play up to now as participants in a collective, shared experience. As we saw above (Act 4, scene 1, line 197) though, that is not quite how they themselves have experienced it.

A Midsummer Night's Dream is not just about a collection of individuals: it contains three different classes whose lives have been separate, except for colliding at certain crucial points. At the top of this hierarchy is (1) the world of Oberon and Titania: Fairyland. Below that is the mortal world, which naturally seems to subdivide itself: (2), the aristocratic class that contains Theseus, Hippolyta, Egeus and the young lovers, seems so far removed from (3), the class comprised by the *mechanicals*, that they might as well be in different worlds.

We have already seen how the fallout from Oberon and Titania's marital disputes has affected events in the human world. We have seen it affecting the young lovers, who happened to stray into the wood on a night when Oberon was at large with magic on his mind. Worlds 1 and 3 have seriously collided only once, in Titania's ludicrous love for the transformed Bottom. But it is an interesting comment on the social order within the play that, as of the end of Act 4, Worlds 2 and 3 have yet to meet at all. Bottom, Quince and company might have been in a different play altogether from Theseus, Hippolyta and the young lovers, for all the contact they have had up to now.

take a break before the grand finale

Act 5 *scene* 1

◆ The next evening, Theseus and Hippolyta discuss the doings of the night before.
◆ Egeus announces the entertainments on offer. Theseus chooses *Pyramus and Thisbe*.
◆ The play is a shambles, but still good-humouredly received.
◆ Theseus brings the celebrations to a close and the mortals go off to bed.
◆ Oberon, Titania and Puck bless the house and the newly-wed couples.

This scene finds us back in Athens, the dreams of the past night now firmly in the past. As far as Theseus is concerned, indeed, they never even happened, for he is profoundly sceptical about the lovers' story. *The lunatic, the lover and the poet*, he says, *Are of imagination all compact*. Within the world of the play, we know, he is wrong: these marvels really did take place.

For us, however, his words have their implications. The three categories share a tendency to project the contents of their fantasy onto the world. The lunatic, in his delusions, peoples his world with demons; the lover thinks his beloved beautiful however hideous the reality; the poet weaves whole worlds out of *airy nothing* – as of course the author of *A Midsummer Night's Dream* has done. *Such tricks hath strong imagination*, argues Theseus:

> *That if it would but apprehend some joy*
> *It comprehends the bringer of that joy;*
> *Or in the night, imagining some fear,*
> *How easy is a bush supposed a bear.*
> (lines 18–23)

If we let the imagination have its way, says Theseus, we let our wishes and fears colour our view of reality. But can any of us really avoid doing this, every day of our lives? Theseus's rationalism is when you think about it every bit as distorting, blinding him as it does to what we know – within the world of the play, at least – has truly taken place.

 STYLE AND LANGUAGE

We have seen how, for much of the play, the aristocrats in the cast have tended to speak in verse, the lower-class workmen in prose. Here this tendency is reversed, the prose comments of the Duke and his friends throwing into relief the actors' unaccustomed verse-speaking. And it is unaccustomed: look how mixed up Quince gets in his prologue, confused as he is between line-ends and sentence-breaks.

Whatever illusion there may be in this play-within-the-play is stretched to the limits by its audience's little observations throughout, but is of course completely shattered when Bottom, hearing Theseus's observation at line 180, breaks off to put him right (line 181). The illusion keeps being suspended during this performance: it will be deliberately broken in Snug's speech as gentle lion (lines 217–24), in the interests of reassuring the ladies in the audience, and collapse through sheer vexation later (lines 252–4) when Starveling, tired of trying to deliver his lines through his audience's relentless heckling, lapses into exasperated prose.

Once again, these players' failure to understand the conventions of theatre make us think a little harder about how those conventions work for us. Theseus sums it up (lines 210–11), when Hippolyta dismisses the whole show as silly: *The best in this kind are but shadows, and the worst are no worse if imagination amend them.* The audience's imagination is having to work overtime to 'amend' matters here, of course

– but Theseus is right: no play can hope to do without it completely, not even one of Shakespeare's!

The play ended, Theseus packs the lovers off to bed, an order which creates a strict demarcation between day and night. We said before that it was significant that Theseus had taken no part in the central, night-time wood section of the play. Now, he says, midnight has struck: it is *almost fairy time*. Given his comments at the start of this scene, it seems likely that this is a joking remark: having seen the play unfolding, however, we know it is truer than he realises.

PUCK HAS THE LAST WORD

As if on cue, Puck appears, his speech, like his earlier one at Act 3, scene 2, lines 380–7, laying emphasis on the negative side of night (how different his lion is to Snug's, for example!) but reminding the audience that there are good fairies, too, who will see that all in Theseus's house are kept safe from harm. For a speech of reassurance, it is a little odd. While it is nice to know that the fairies are going to be providing protection, is it not unsettling to be reminded quite so vividly as this of the terrors they are going to be protecting the household *from*? Oberon's speech, too – with its references to the kind of disfigurements which *could* afflict the couples' children – is as disturbing as it is soothing. ❂ How might you edit it to make it more reassuring?

The main point is, though, that the action will conclude with its gaze fixed firmly on the future. Life will go on holding its fears and its dangers, but it *will* go on, that is the main thing. This closing scene has been an opening scene as well, bringing together every category of character who has appeared in the play – court, commoners and immortals alike – to celebrate a grand collective marriage and hence the start of a new generation.

In describing the spirits as *shadows*, Puck's closing speech echoes the remarks Theseus makes earlier in the scene (line 210) about the theatrical illusion (*The best in this kind are but shadows* ...). As he goes on, Puck blurs the distinction between night and day, weaving together ever more closely the idea of theatre, enchantment and dream:

Think but this, and all is mended:
That you have but slumbered here,
While these visions did appear;

His remark about the *serpent's tongue* – an audience's hiss of
disapproval – seems to bring us out of the dream and return us
to the theatre, where a play has just finished. Yet the image
also reminds us of the serpent which shed its skin on Titania's
bank (Act 2, scene 1, line 255), the one which attacked
Hermia in her dream-within-the-dream (Act 3, scene 1, lines
152–5), and the various other serpents who slide menacingly
through the play and its imagery. If we give Puck a good hand
in applause, though, it is as if we are offering him a hand to
shake in friendship, and so sealing the deal we have made in
accepting the truth of his play.

Your turn

? Bottom's speech, lines 168–75, is obviously terrible
stuff, but why exactly? Look at it more closely: what
effects was the author of *Pyramus and Thisbe* trying to
achieve here, and where did it all go wrong? How
about his speech in lines 266–81 when he finds the
mantle? And Flute's, as Thisbe (lines 318–41): why
does this seem so ridiculously un-tragic? Think about
line-lengths, rhyme, rhythm and the use of particular
words. (Look in particular at the comparisons this
speech gives for Pyramus's features: how appropriate
do you think they are?)

TOPICS FOR DISCUSSION AND BRAINSTORMING

One of the best ways to revise is with one or more friends. Even if you're with someone who hardly knows the text you're studying, you'll find that having to explain things to your friend will help you to organise your own thoughts and memorise key points. If you're with someone who has studied the text, you'll find that the things you can't remember are different from the things your friend can't remember – so you'll be able to help each other.

Discussion will also help you to develop interesting new ideas that perhaps neither of you would have had alone. Use a **brainstorming** approach to tackle any of the topics listed below. Allow yourself to share whatever ideas come into your head – however silly they seem. This will get you thinking creatively.

Whether alone or with a friend, use Mind Mapping (see p. v) to help you brainstorm and organise your ideas. If with a friend, use a large sheet of paper and coloured pens.

TOPICS

1 Now you know *A Midsummer Night's Dream* so well, how about rewriting it? You (and your friend) could try retelling the story of the play from the point of view of one of its characters. That isn't as easy as it sounds: remember, not everybody shares the same experience. Theseus never goes into the night-time wood, for instance. Also, as a Duke, whom everybody has to look up to, he has a very different perspective to that of a young girl like Hermia, who has to (or at least who is supposed to!) just do as she is told. Lysander and Peter Quince both have their own very different way with words: how might each describe the *Pyramus and Thisbe* performance in Act 5, scene 1? And how would Bottom's perspective on things compare with that of a more educated character like Demetrius? Or a less innocent one like Puck? Find lines in the text to support your view of what their view would be. Choose a character and try it now.

2 How do the different social groups in *A Midsummer Night's Dream* differ from each other, reflect each other, and perceive each other?

3 Discuss how authority is presented in *A Midsummer Night's Dream*.

4 What transformations take place in *A Midsummer Night's Dream*, and how are they significant?

5 How are the different settings important in *A Midsummer Night's Dream*?

6 What aspects of love can you identify in the play? Use the illustration on p. 74 help you.

7 How many different verse forms can you find in the play? What reasons can you see for the variations? In Shakespeare's blank verse, can you find lines which depart from the rigid (iambic pentameter) norm? In each case, why do you think Shakespeare has done this?

8 What part does humour play? Is the clownish comedy just there for 'light relief' – or does it tell us something more serious about human life?

9 The moon is an important image in *A Midsummer Night's Dream*. Because the old moon gradually grew fat then produced a tiny new one, the ancients associated it with pregnancy, birth and death; its dazzling whiteness, on the other hand, made them think of maiden chastity. These paradoxical qualities can both be found in *A Midsummer Night's Dream*, as can the sheer sense of atmosphere moonlight creates. Trace the image of the moon through the play: what roles do you see it playing?

10 What different things does magic mean in *A Midsummer Night's Dream*?

11 For immortals, Oberon and Puck are particularly prone to what we call 'human error': why might this be, and what do you think it tells us?

12 Think about the different roles that men and women have in the play: do you see any patterns emerging? Who's in charge – and who does Shakespeare think should be?

Any of these topics could feature in an exam paper, but even if you think you've found one in your actual exam, be sure to answer the precise question given.

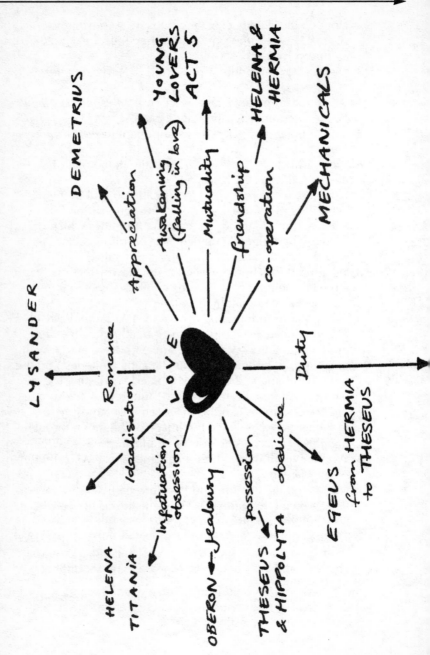

LYSANDER

DEMETRIUS

YOUNG LOVERS ACT 5

HELENA & HERMIA

MECHANICALS

Appreciation

Awakening (falling in love)

Mutuality

friendship

co-operation

Romance

LOVE

Duty

Idealisation

Infatuation/obsession

Jealousy

possession

obedience

from HERMIA to THESEUS

HELENA TITANIA

OBERON

THESEUS & HIPPOLYTA

EGEUS

74

Ow to get an 'A' in English Literature

In all your study, in coursework, and in exams, be aware of the following:

- **Characterisation** – the characters and how we know about them (e.g. what they say and do, how the author describes them), their relationships, and how they develop.
- **Plot and structure** – what happens and how it is organised into parts or episodes.
- **Setting and atmosphere** – the changing scene and how it reflects the story (e.g. the use of the city of Athens and the wood to reflect reality and dream).
- **Style and language** – the author's choice of words, and literary devices such as imagery, and how these reflect the mood.
- **Viewpoint** – how the story is told (e.g. through an imaginary narrator, or in the third person but through the eyes of one character – 'She was furious – how dare he!').
- **Social and historical context** – influences on the author (see 'Background' in this guide).

Develop your ability to:

- Relate **detail** to **broader content, meaning and style**.
- Show understanding of the author's **intentions, technique and meaning** (brief and appropriate comparisons with other works by the same author will gain marks).
- Give **personal response and interpretation**, backed up by **examples** and short **quotations**. (Use short, appropriate quotations as 'evidence' of your understanding of that part of the text – don't just stick large chunks down for the sake of it!)
- **Evaluate** the author's achievement (how far does the author succeed and why?)
- Use literary terms to show your understanding of what the author is trying to achieve with language.

You will probably have about an hour for one essay. It is worth spending about 10 minutes planning it. An excellent way to do this is in the three stages below.

1 **Mind Map** your ideas, without worrying about the order yet.
2 **Order** the relevant ideas (the ones that really relate to the question) by numbering them in the order in which you will write the essay.
3 **Gather** your evidence and short quotes.

You could remember this as the **MOG** technique.

Model answer and essay plan

The next (and final) chapter consists of a model answer to an exam question on *A Midsummer Night's Dream*, together with the Mind Map and essay plan used to write it. Don't be put off if you don't think you could write an essay to this standard yet. You'll develop your skills if you work at them. Even if you're reading this the night before your exam, you can easily memorise the MOG technique in order to do your personal best.

The model answer and essay plan are good examples for you to follow, but don't try to learn them off by heart. It's better to pay close attention to the wording of the question you choose to answer in the exam, and allow Mind Mapping to help you to think creatively.

Before reading the answer, you might like to do a plan of your own, then compare it with the example. The numbered points, with comments at the end, show why it's a good answer.

M ODEL ANSWER AND ESSAY PLAN

QUESTION

Explain how Shakespeare underlines the differences between the mortal and the immortal worlds in *A Midsummer Night's Dream*. Refer particularly to Act 3 scene 2, from line 122 to the end, where Titania falls in love with Bottom.

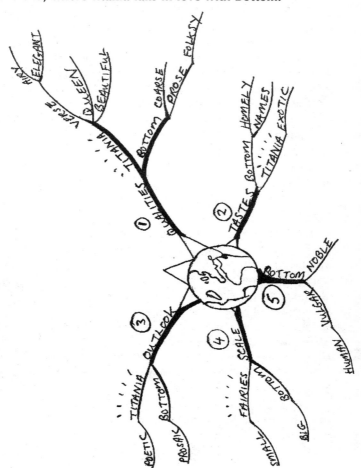

PLAN

Bottom: bottom – mortal, not just earthly but down-to-earth.
Titania: top – immortal, romantic, away with the fairies

1 Bottom: coarse commoner with simple prose style:
   references to common things (birds) in familiar, folksy
   vocabulary (proverbs).
   Titania: beautiful queen, elegant and sophisticated in
   speech. Smooth, regular verse, long words, sacred (angel),
   airy and delicate things (flowers).
2 Differences in tastes. Bottom: homely, hearty food
   Titania: exotic delicacies (apricots, grapes, figs)
   (NB Bottom's earthy interpretations of delicate names of
   fairy servants (different associations of cobweb,
   mustardseed, etc).)
3 Confusion of scale: big Bottom – miniature fairies.
4 Romantic versus realistic outlooks: Titania's poetic praises
   contrast (comically) with Bottom's prosaic reality.
5 Bottom's clumsiness and vulgarity stands for earthly
   limitations of humankind in general – but also a touch of
   nobility.

ESSAY

The differences between the two worlds, the mortal and the
immortal, are evident even in the different sorts of language
Bottom and Titania use. Bottom's earthiness is shown by the
fact that he speaks in simple prose – except for where he sings
a song. Even then it is a song about familiar, unexotic birds
(the ousel or blackbird, the 'throstle' or thrush, the 'wren', the
'finch', the 'sparrow' ...) and its short, rhyming lines make it
seem very unsophisticated.[1] In the theatre the actor playing
Bottom might sing this song in a raucous, braying voice.[2] This
would be comically appropriate given Bottom's ass's head, but
would also contrast amusingly with the sweet voices of the
songbirds he is singing about. Bottom uses homely expressions
like 'methinks' and 'not so, neither' – even slightly vulgar-
sounding ones such as 'gleek'.

Titania, by contrast, speaks in smooth, regular verse. In the
theatre, the gentleness of the actress's delivery might
emphasise this contrast with Bottom's harsh voice. And where
Bottom talked of common songbirds, she speaks of mysterious,

sacred things ('angel') and beautiful, delicate ones ('flow'ry bed'). Her language sounds much more educated than Bottom's: she uses words like 'enamoured' and 'enthrallèd' and employs clever turns of phrase ('And thy fair virtue's force perforce doth move me').[3]

Bottom's instincts always seem to be physical. The names of Titania's fairies all suggest lightness and miniature size, but Bottom always latches on to more down-to-earth associations of these names. Instead of thinking of a cobweb's beautiful thinness, he thinks of its everyday use like a plaster to heal a cut finger; rather than think of the tiny size of a mustardseed, he greedily imagines a great joint of beef. And it is not only that he thinks about food rather than higher things. Even when he is thinking about food, the humble foodstuffs he imagines, such as 'ox-beef' and peas, contrast with the exotic delicacies – 'apricots, grapes' and 'figs' – which Titania promises him.[4]

This scene throws our sense of scale into confusion, which further highlights the differences between the mortal and immortal worlds. Titania's instruction to her fairies to 'gambol' in Bottom's eyes emphasises not only their microscopic size but their weightlessness: if their frolics will not irritate even this most sensitive part of Bottom's body, they really must be 'airy' spirits. The queen's fairies 'will the honeybags steal from the humble-bees', she says, use their 'waxen thighs' for 'night tapers' and 'light them at the fiery glow-worms's eyes'. All of this suggests a miniature smallness of scale which is at odds with Bottom's brash clumsiness. But Bottom talks to them very naturally, as if they were ordinary, life-sized people. Our confusion is increased by the fact that these spirits also operate on a larger scale than we can imagine Bottom doing: they will fetch 'jewels from the deep', Titania promises, which implies the covering of vast distances. It also means that they can function in environments ('the deep') where Bottom would be out of his element. These fairies make a nonsense of our ideas of scale. Just as Puck, earlier in the play, could 'put a girdle round about the earth / In forty minutes, they are not bound by human limitations.'[5]

The contrast between Titania's extravagant praises and Bottom's obvious unworthiness of them forms the basis for much of the humour of this scene. When Bottom has delivered a bit of what sounds like hackneyed 'homespun' proverbial wisdom ('reason and love keep little company together nowadays – the more the pity that some honest neighbours will not make them friends') she responds by saying: 'Thou art as wise as thou art beautiful.'[6] There is an enjoyable irony in this comment: Bottom may indeed be as wise as he is beautiful but then, especially with his ass's head, that is not saying very much![7]

The humour in this scene also serves a more serious purpose, however: Titania's contrast between Bottom's 'mortal grossness' and 'an airy spirit' reminds us that, though in his ludicrous clumsiness and vulgarity Bottom is an extreme case, all mortals are bound by their physical bodies. However refined we were, we would all seem 'gross' next to an 'airy' spirit. The ass's head which Puck has given Bottom can be seen as standing for the earthbound, animal nature in all of us, as against the airy freedom of the spirits. At the same time, though, Bottom's basic good-heartedness, which shines through in the friendly courtesy and kindness he shows to his new servants, reminds us of the nobility of which we as humans are capable.[8] With dazzling grace and enjoyable humour, therefore, and without apparently attempting to teach us anything, Shakespeare has brilliantly captured in a single scene both our limitations and our possibilities as human beings.

WHAT'S SO GOOD ABOUT IT?

1 Shows an awareness of how *content* (the ideas Shakespeare is trying to convey to us, the impression he wants us to get) is reflected in *form* – the way he chooses to present these ideas (style and language).
2 Shows an awareness of the play as theatre.
3 Shows appreciation of differences in language.
4 This paragraph gives several good examples to back up the clearly worded statement with which it begins.
5 This paragraph nicely summarises Shakespeare's use of difference in size and distance.
6 Good use of quotations.
7 Shows appreciation of the subtler points of Shakespeare's humour.
8 As the essay approaches its conclusion it moves out from the line-by-line detail of the scene to the big picture, considering the general truths the scene has seemed to embody.

alliteration   repetition of a sound at the beginnings of words, e.g. *The raging rocks/And shivering shocks* (Act 1, scene 2, lines 25–6).

aside   a short speech spoken by one character, as if thinking aloud, not meant to be heard by others on stage.

blank verse   the kind of non-rhyming verse in which Shakespeare usually writes, with five pairs of syllables to a line, with the stress always on the second syllable; unrhymed iambic pentameter (see p. xii).

context   the social and historical influences on the author.

couplet   *see* **rhyming couplet**.

dramatic irony   *see* **irony (dramatic)**

foreshadowing   an indirect warning of things to come, often through imagery.

iambic pentameter   verse with five pairs of syllables to a line, with the stress always on the second syllable.

image   a word picture used to make an idea come alive; e.g. a **metaphor**, **simile**, or **personification** (see separate entries).

imagery   the kind of word picture used to make an idea come alive.

irony   **(dramatic)** where at least one character on stage is unaware of an important fact which the audience knows about, and which is somehow hinted at; **(simple)** where a character says the opposite of what they really think, or pretends to be ignorant of the true facts, usually to show scorn or ridicule.

metaphor   a description of a thing as if it were something essentially different but also in some way similar; e.g. . . . *we must starve our sight/From lovers' food* (Act 1, scene 1, lines 222–3).

personification a description of something as if it were a person; e.g . . . *angry winter* (Act 2, scene 1, line 112).

prose language in which, unlike verse, there is no set number of syllables in a line, and no rhyming.

pun a use of a word with two meanings, or of two similar-sounding words, where both meanings are appropriate in different ways.

rhetoric the art of effective or persuasive speaking or writing.

rhyming couplet a pair of rhyming lines, often used at the end of a speech.

setting the place in which the action occurs, usually affecting the atmosphere; e.g. Athens, or the wood.

simile a comparison of two things which are different in most ways but similar in one important way; e.g. *So we grew together,/Like to a double cherry* (Act 3, scene 2, lines 208–9).

soliloquy a speech spoken by an actor alone on stage as if thinking aloud.

structure how the plot is organised.

theme an idea explored by an author; e.g. perception.

tragedy a play focusing on a tragic hero or couple (e.g. *Pyramus and Thisbe*).

tragic hero a character whose nobility or achievement we admire, and whose downfall and death through a weakness or error, coupled with fate, arouses our sympathy.

viewpoint how the story is told; e.g. through action, or in discussion between minor characters.

INDEX